BARBARIANS AND THE BIRTH OF CHINESE IDENTITY

The Five Dynasties and Ten Kingdoms to the Yuan Dynasty (907 – 1368)

Jing Liu

UNDERSTANDING

CHINA

THROUGH COMICS

VOLUME 3

A GRAPHIC NOVEL HISTORY FROM STONE BRIDGE PRESS

Berkeley CA

Published by
STONE BRIDGE PRESS
P.O. Box 8208 · Berkeley, California 94707
TEL 510-524-8732 · sbp@stonebridge.com · www.stonebridge.com

First edition, 2017.

First on-demand edition, 2023.

Book design and layout by Linda Ronan.

Printed in the United States of America.

LIBRARY OF CONGRESS CATALOGING-IN-PUBLICATION DATA
Names: Liu, Jing (Author of graphic novels), author, illustrator.
Title: Foundations of Chinese civilization / Jing Liu.
Description: First edition. | Berkeley : Stone Bridge Press, 2016. | Series:
  Understanding China through comics | Includes bibliographical references
  and index.
Identifiers: LCCN 2016009755 (print) | LCCN 2016012382 (ebook) | ISBN
  9781611720273 (alk. paper) | ISBN 9781611729184 (ebook)
Subjects: LCSH: China—History—Comic books, strips, etc. | Graphic novels.
Classification: LCC DS735 .L576 2016 (print) | LCC DS735 (ebook) | DDC
  931—dc23
LC record available at http://lccn.loc.gov/2016009755

pISBN 978-1-61172-034-1
eISBN 978-1-61172-926-9

CONTENTS

TIMELINE

907 — —Five Dynasties and Ten Kingdoms period begins
—Khitan tribes establish the Liao dynasty

960 — —Five Dynasties and Ten Kingdoms period ends and Song dynasty established

1038 — —Tangut tribes establish the Western Xia dynasty

1069 — —Wang Anshi begins New Policy reforms

1081 — —Song dynasty launches invasion of Xia dynasty

1115 — —Jurchen tribes establish Jin dynasty

1125 — —Liao dynasty collapses

1127 — —Southern Song dynasty established

1141 — —Jin and Southern Song dynasties sign Treaty of Shaoxing

1200 — —Zhu Xi, a Neo-Confucian philosopher, dies

1206 — —Temujin takes title of Genghis Khan after uniting Mongol tribes

1211 — —Mongols defeat Jin dynasty at Battle of Badger Mouth

1227 — —Xia dynasty collapses

1234 — —Jin dynasty collapses

1257 — —Mongols launch invasion of Southern Song dynasty

1271 — —Yuan dynasty established by Kublai Khan

1279 — —Yuan and Southern Song dynasties meet at Battle of Yamen
—Southern Song dynasty collapses

1281 — —Yuan dynasty launches invasion of Japan

1294 — —Kublai Khan dies

1295 — —Marco Polo returns to Italy

1351 — —Rebellions against Yuan dynasty

INTRODUCTION

Trying to disentangle, let alone understand, the long history of China is not for the faint of heart. The labyrinth of Chinese dynasties, intertwined ethnicities, and gigantic land mass can put off the adventurer to this fascinating nation. We need help to explore and explain how this country came to be. Jing Liu has done us a great service in his Understanding China through Comics series. Not only has he made China's history accessible to us, but he has done so with both wit and charm. On top of that, he has offered us lively visual and concrete vignettes that stick in the mind, mapping pivotal events in space and time.

In Volume 3, *Barbarians and the Birth of Chinese Identity*, Jing Liu continues to lead us on this expedition to discover what historical treasures lie beneath the dust of Chinese history. We discover the vibrant life of the middle period of the China story—the Northern and Southern Song dynasties, and the invasion and conquests by the Mongols under Genghis Khan and his descendants. This formative period was racked by wars, but at the same time, and as we watch in these pages, it produced innovation, commerce, and cultural accomplishments that defined the Chinese nation. Dive into the history of this period. You will not be disappointed.

David M Jacobson, historian, quarter-century resident of China, foreign expert for the Chinese Academy of Social Sciences and Northeast Normal University

Previously in
Understanding China through Comics

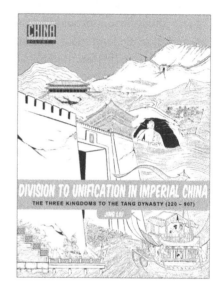

Volume 1

Foundations of
Chinese Civilization:
The Yellow Emperor
to the Han Dynasty
(2697 BCE – 220 CE)

Volume 2

Division to Unification
in Imperial China:
The Three Kingdoms to
the Tang Dynasty
(220 – 907)

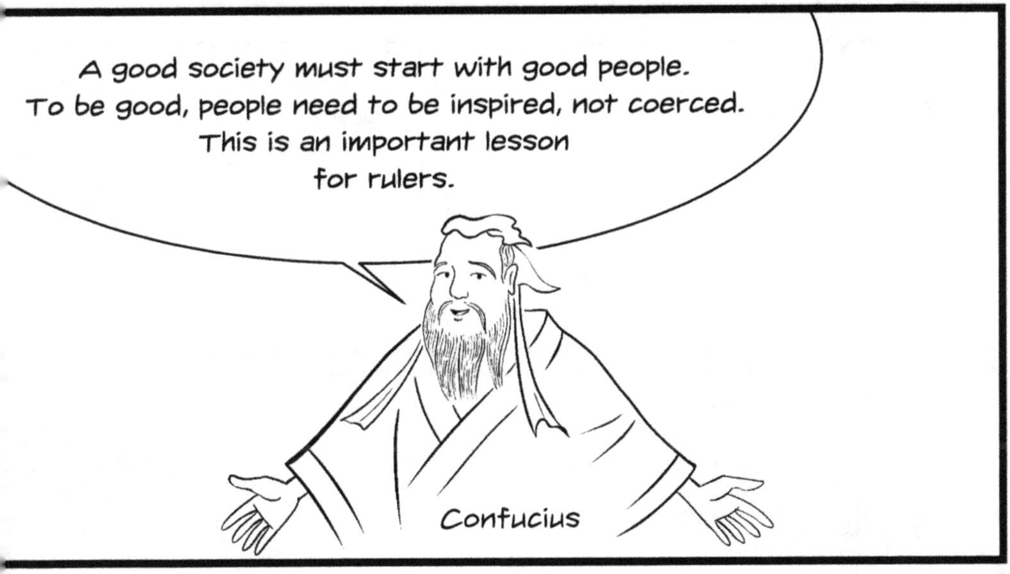
A good society must start with good people. To be good, people need to be inspired, not coerced. This is an important lesson for rulers.
Confucius

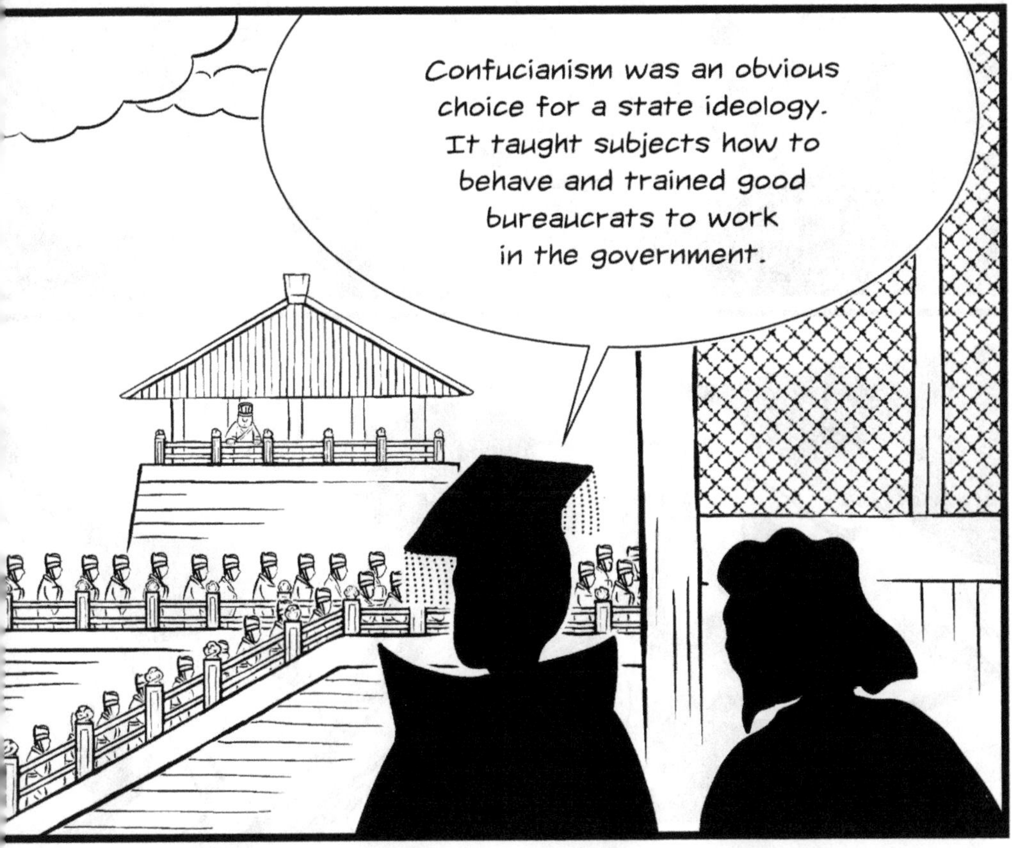
Confucianism was an obvious choice for a state ideology. It taught subjects how to behave and trained good bureaucrats to work in the government.

But often officials supposed to be serving the emperor used their positions in the court to take power for themselves. They were corrupt and the people suffered as a result.

Down with the dynasty!

As dynasties rose and fell, a pattern was established that would persist throughout Chinese history. First dynasties prospered, then grew corrupt, and finally collapsed.

Sometimes new dynasties would reunite China right away. Other times China would remain divided. When the Han dynasty fell in 220 CE, China entered the Age of Division, a period of time that lasted for 400 years.

During the Age of Division, commoners were faced with many hardships.

In this time of widespread suffering, Buddhism, a religion from India, offered a remedy to the pain of the common person that was radically different from more traditional Chinese solutions.

Why is there so much suffering?

Confucianism:

We will build a good government to end the suffering.

Taoism:

Suffering is an inescapable aspect of human life. Learn to live with it.

Buddhism:

Yes, suffering is part of life. But you can end it!

Practice spiritual exercises to detach yourself from desire. Desire is the source of suffering.

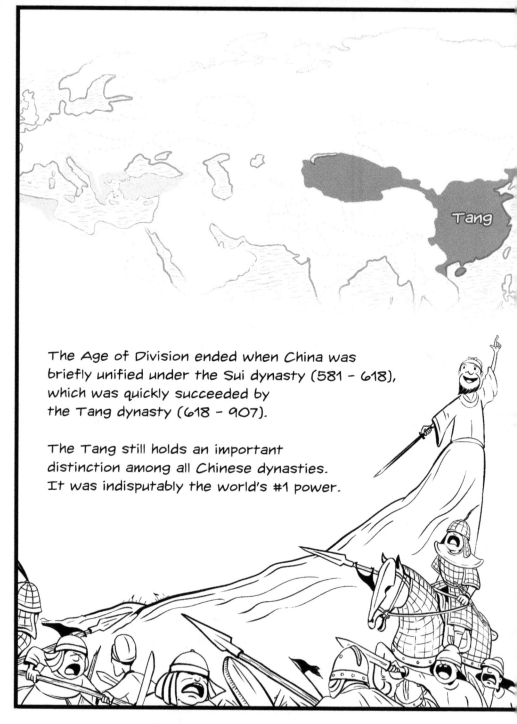

The Age of Division ended when China was briefly unified under the Sui dynasty (581 – 618), which was quickly succeeded by the Tang dynasty (618 – 907).

The Tang still holds an important distinction among all Chinese dynasties. It was indisputably the world's #1 power.

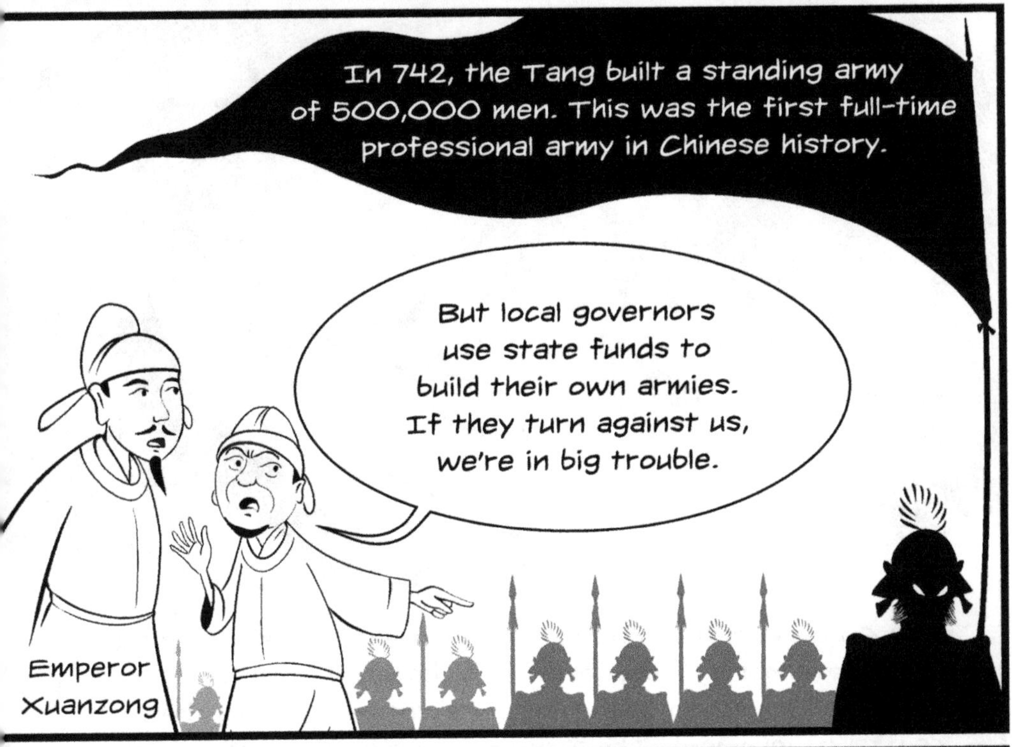
In 742, the Tang built a standing army of 500,000 men. This was the first full-time professional army in Chinese history.
But local governors use state funds to build their own armies. If they turn against us, we're in big trouble.
Emperor Xuanzong

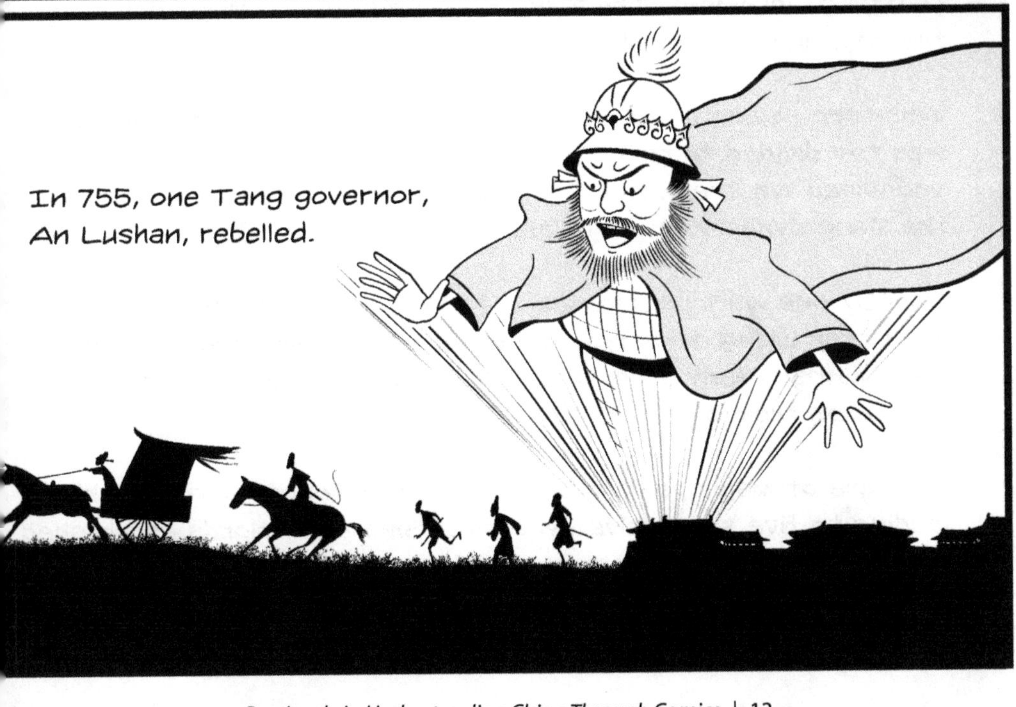
In 755, one Tang governor, An Lushan, rebelled.

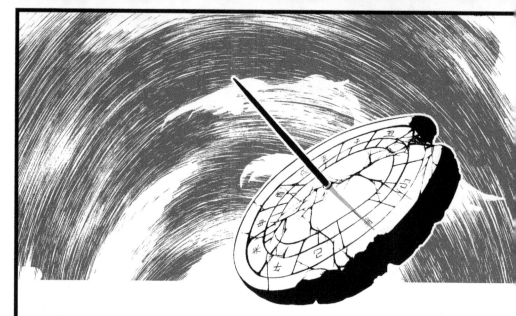

The An Lushan rebellion was crushed with the help of other
Tang governors. These governors, however, then used their
newfound power to gain even more autonomy from the
central government. The Tang remained decentralized for
the next 100 years.

When the Huang Chao rebellion broke out in 874, the country
was too divided to restore order. The rebellion lasted 10 years
and wiped out the entire Chinese aristocracy, the foundation of
the Tang dynasty's ruling class.

In 907 one warlord deposed the Tang and established
the Later Liang dynasty, without fully reunifying the rest of
the country. Many other Tang governors simply continued
to rule on their own.

A couple of major powers battled for control of northern China,
leading to five successive dynasties. Smaller warlords established
a dozen rival states, most in southern China. This period of time
is now known as the Five Dynasties and Ten Kingdoms.

UNDERSTANDING
CHINA
THROUGH COMICS

Volume

3

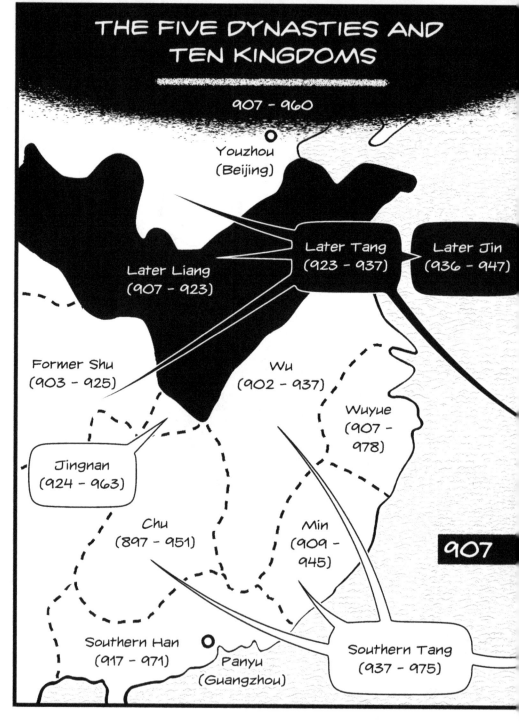

THE FIVE DYNASTIES AND TEN KINGDOMS

907 - 960

Youzhou
(Beijing)

Later Tang
(923 - 937)

Later Jin
(936 - 947)

Later Liang
(907 - 923)

Former Shu
(903 - 925)

Wu
(902 - 937)

Wuyue
(907 - 978)

Jingnan
(924 - 963)

Chu
(897 - 951)

Min
(909 - 945)

907

Southern Han
(917 - 971)

Panyu
(Guangzhou)

Southern Tang
(937 - 975)

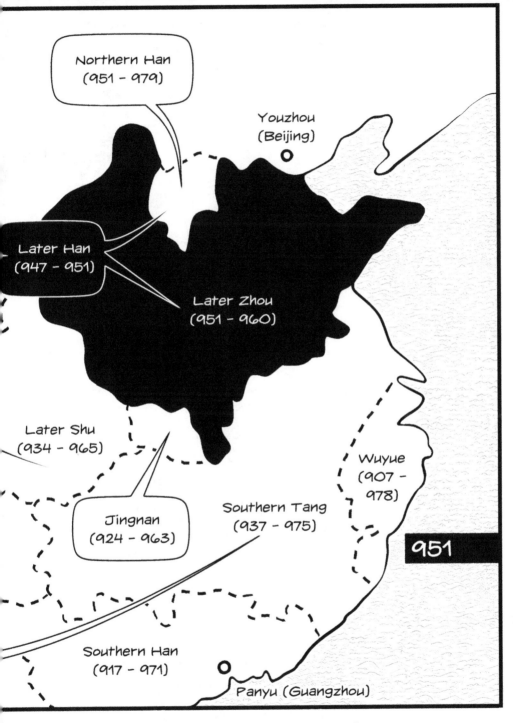

Northern Han
(951 – 979)

Youzhou
(Beijing)

Later Han
(947 – 951)

Later Zhou
(951 – 960)

Later Shu
(934 – 965)

Wuyue
(907 –
978)

Jingnan
(924 – 963)

Southern Tang
(937 – 975)

951

Southern Han
(917 – 971)

Panyu (Guangzhou)

During the Five Dynasties and Ten Kingdoms period states were ruled by warlords constantly looking to engage their rivals in battle. Generals would sell their armies to anyone with enough money.

This violence came at great cost. Warring states would breach the Yellow River dyke in an attempt to defeat their rivals, causing 24 massive floods in only 53 years.

The Khitans and the Great Wall

Several embattled states sought help from a Khitan kingdom, also known as the Liao dynasty (907 – 1125).

The Khitans were descendants of the Xianbei people in northeast Asia. They rose to prominence with the unification of various Khitan tribes in 907.

However, the Khitans had their own plans.
They pitted Chinese warlords against each other,
defeating three of the five dynasties in northern China.
They took control of the Great Wall, the last defense
of the Chinese heartland.

In 938, the Liao constructed a capital city close to modern-day Beijing.

Beijing is a capital city for the first time in Chinese history.

It's a convenient location from which to launch our annual raids on China.

Liao

Later Zhou

Sixteen Prefectures or the Great Wall region

Liao Southern Capital (Beijing)

The rise of Zhao Kuangyin

In 954, the Liao invaded the Later Zhou. Both sides met near the city of Gaoping.

Attack!

Order our reinforcements to hurry up! We have to hold the line until they arrive.

Emperor Shizong of Later Zhou (921 – 959)

The right flank of the Later Zhou army collapsed.
Many generals fled the battle.
Thousands of soldiers surrendered.

But one cavalry officer held strong, charging forward with 2,000 elite palace troops and keeping the Liao forces at bay.

Zhao Kuangyin
(927 - 976)

Hours passed.

Our reinforcements have arrived!

The Later Zhou won.
This victory marked the first successful attempt by the Chinese to defeat a Khitan incursion following the fall of the Tang.

The battle of Gaoping earned Zhao Kuangyin much recognition and the title of Chief Commander of the Palace Troops of the Later Zhou. After Emperor Shizong of Later Zhou died, Zhao established the Song dynasty. In 20 years, the Song unified most of China.

THE SONG DYNASTY

960 – 1279

Capital Bianjing
(Kaifeng)

Song

Failed attempts against the Liao

The Song army tried to retake the Great Wall from the Liao, reaching as far as the Liao Capital.

However, the Liao had learned much from Chinese civilization, having occupied parts of northern China for decades. They knew how to organize a large population, manage agriculture, and build walled cities to withstand long sieges.
They were fearsome foes.

After years of fighting, neither side could gain the upper hand. A peace treaty was signed in 1005.

The Song will send us an annual tribute: 200,000 bolts of silk and 100,000 ounces of silver.

The tribute is less than 2% of what we would have spent for wars against the Liao.

At the height of the Song-Liao war, the Tangut tribe sided with the Liao. They went on to establish the Western Xia dynasty (1038 – 1227) decades later.

The Tanguts came from multiple ethnic groups including Xianbei and Tibetan peoples.

Compromise with the Western Xia

The Xia dynasty held the Silk Road, which allowed them to control the trade of horses, a crucial military resource.

A blockade by the Xia prevented the Song dynasty from obtaining more warhorses. In the early days of the dynasty, the Song had 170,000 horses. Over the years that number dropped due to wars and a shortage of supply. At the lowest point in 1102, the Song only had 1,800 horses.

By comparison, the Han dynasty had 600,000, and the Tang 706,000.

To secure a more steady supply of horses, the Song tried to take the Xia trading routes by force. After years of costly wars, the two states made peace in 1044.

We recognize the Song as our overlord in exchange for receiving annual gifts of 50,000 ounces of silver, 130,000 bolts of silk, and 20,000 catties of tea.

And don't forget the holiday bonus: 22,000 ounces of silver, 23,000 bolts of silk, and 10,000 catties of tea.

When we were fighting the Western Xia our annual military expenses were 70 times more than these annual gifts.

At this point China was divided into three dynasties.

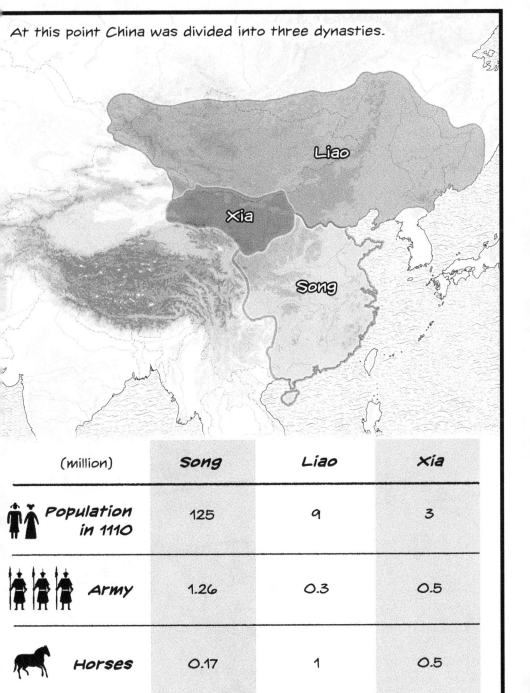

(million)	Song	Liao	Xia
Population in 1110	125	9	3
Army	1.26	0.3	0.5
Horses	0.17	1	0.5

New Policy reforms

Conflicts with the Liao and Xia cost the Song dearly.

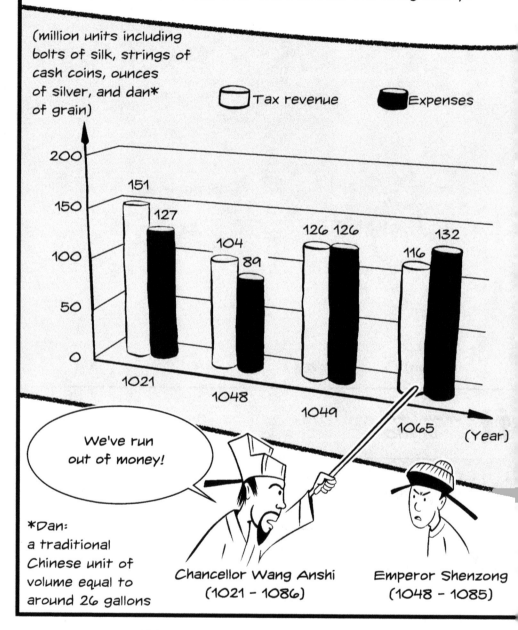

30 | BARBARIANS AND THE BIRTH OF CHINESE IDENTITY

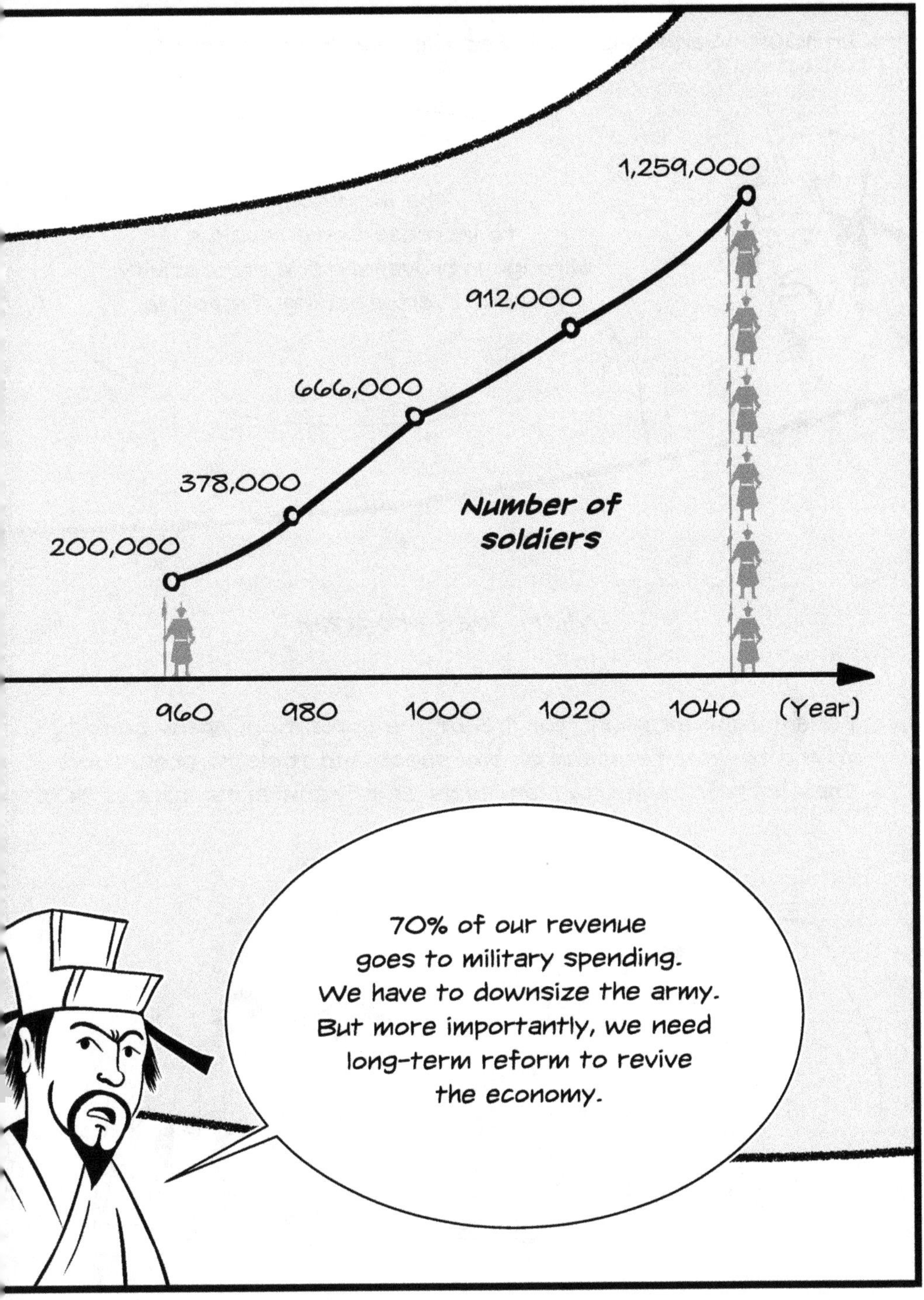
1,259,000
912,000
666,000
378,000
200,000
Number of soldiers
960
980
1000
1020
1040
(Year)
70% of our revenue goes to military spending. We have to downsize the army. But more importantly, we need long-term reform to revive the economy.

In 1069, Wang Anshi launched the New Policy reforms.

The main goal is
to increase state revenue
through improvements in productivity,
without overburdening the people.

Micro loan program

Tenant families count for 1/3 of the population. Many can't afford to rent farmland or buy seeds and tools to grow food. They borrow cash from landlords. But the interest rate is 50%!

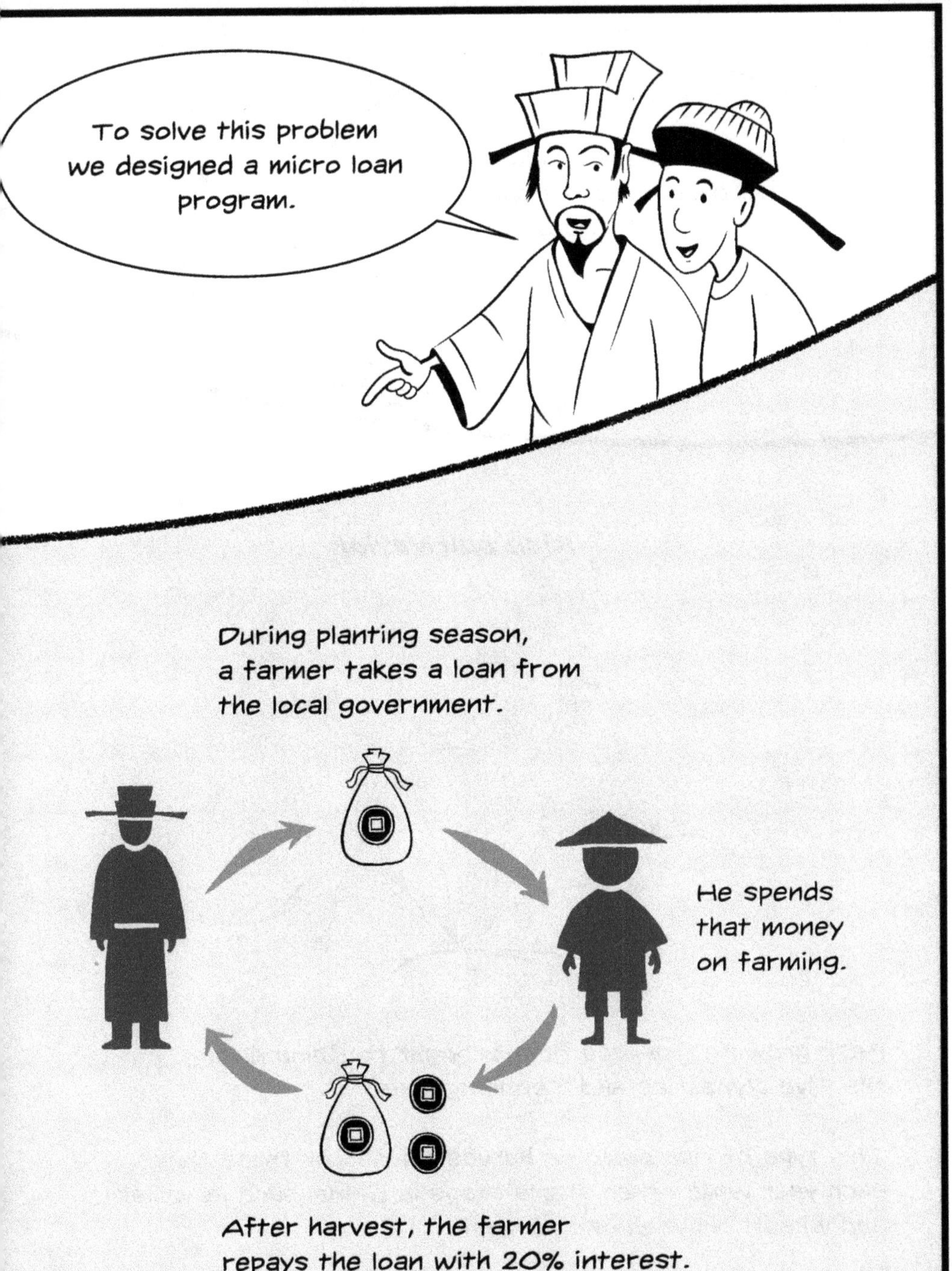
To solve this problem we designed a micro loan program.
During planting season, a farmer takes a loan from the local government.
He spends that money on farming.
After harvest, the farmer repays the loan with 20% interest.

To increase productivity, we encourage the cultivation of rice.

Rice cultivation

Fast-growing rice was first brought to China during the Five Dynasties and Ten Kingdoms.

This type of rice could be harvested two or three times each year while other staple crops in China, such as millet and wheat, only had one harvest.

Growing rice has always been a very labor-intensive business.

- First, remove the topsoil, level the subsoil, and then put the topsoil back. This way the bottom layer of the paddy can hold water, while the surface can provide nutrients that will allow the rice to grow.

- Second, build a dam and channel to flood the paddy and control water.

- Third, plant, weed, fertilize, and harvest the crops.

To improve irrigation systems for growing rice, the Song ordered the construction of more than 10,000 hydraulic projects all over the country.

Hydraulic projects

China's population passed 100 million for the first time thanks to the rice production in southern China.

Before the Song, most dynasties required farmers to provide unpaid labor. This prevented them from having sufficient time to farm. We don't force people to work for free.

Labor law

Farmers can pay a small fee to avoid working for the government.

Local officials collect the money to pay for services.

Imperial examinations

Wang Anshi used imperial exams to recruit the officials he needed to carry out his reforms.

You can spend a lifetime learning fancy words, vague metaphors, and classical poetry. But the country needs people who can think clearly and lead in crisis. Therefore, our exams will focus more on practical skills and less on art and literature.

VARIOUS STATE AGENCIES ARE LOOKING FOR TOP EXAM CANDIDATES TO:

- SET THE PRICE FOR GOODS AND TRADE COMMODITIES TO STABILIZE THE MARKET

- MANAGE PUBLIC ORPHANAGES, HOSPITALS, AND CEMETERIES

The Song tried to make the exams as fair as possible.

Any male adult, regardless of his wealth, can take the exams.

Travel expenses of poor candidates will be paid by the government.

After exams, all answers will be copied by clerks, and test-takers' names will be hidden to avoid preferential treatment.

While privileged families had the money to pay for extensive exam preparation, they still had to compete on a level playing field when it came to taking the test.

Kid, I'll make sure you'll have lots of study time, thousands of books, and professional tutors.

But you must study hard to pass the exam, get a good position in the government, and continue our family legacy.

The examination system reached its peak in the Song.

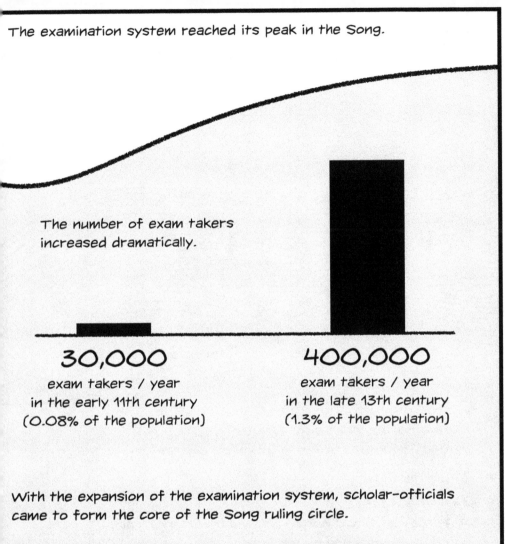

The number of exam takers
increased dramatically.

30,000

exam takers / year
in the early 11th century
(0.08% of the population)

400,000

exam takers / year
in the late 13th century
(1.3% of the population)

With the expansion of the examination system, scholar-officials
came to form the core of the Song ruling circle.

90% of Song chancellors were appointed to their positions
through the examination system, more than in any other dynasty.

50% of Song officials were commoners chosen by
a selection process that rewarded talent as opposed to
family connections.

Many Song scholar-officials went on to become famous figures in Chinese history. Their writings are among the most celebrated works in Chinese literature.

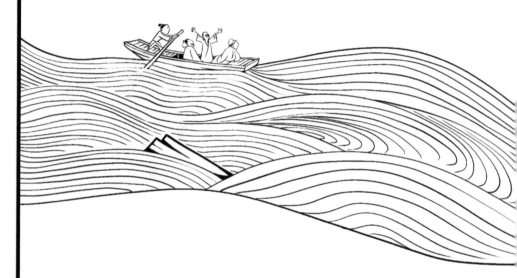

Memorial to Yueyang Tower
by Fan Zhongyan (989 - 1052), Vice Chancellor

不以物喜，不以己悲

A gentleman should not be pleased by external gain, and not be saddened by personal loss.

先天下之忧而忧，后天下之乐而乐

Our first concern should be the country, the last is pleasure.

Pavilion of a Drunken Old Man
by Ouyang Xiu (1007 – 1072), Vice Chancellor

醉翁之意不在酒，在乎山水之间也
The drunkard's heart is not really in the cup,
it belongs to the mountain, the river,
the people and the land.

Reflection at Red Cliff
by Su Shi (1037 – 1101), Minister of Rites

大江东去
浪淘尽
千古风流人物
Thousands of years pass like
a great river flowing eastward.
Waves of time wash away even the biggest man.

Technological advances: gunpowder, the compass, and printing

Wang Anshi was eager to use technology to boost economic growth.

Send qualified candidates to state-run schools to study mathematics, geography, agriculture, medicine, and engineering.

In 10 years, these trained experts had made more than 100 inventions and put them to practical use.

Astronomical clock that displayed information about stars and planets, as well as kept time

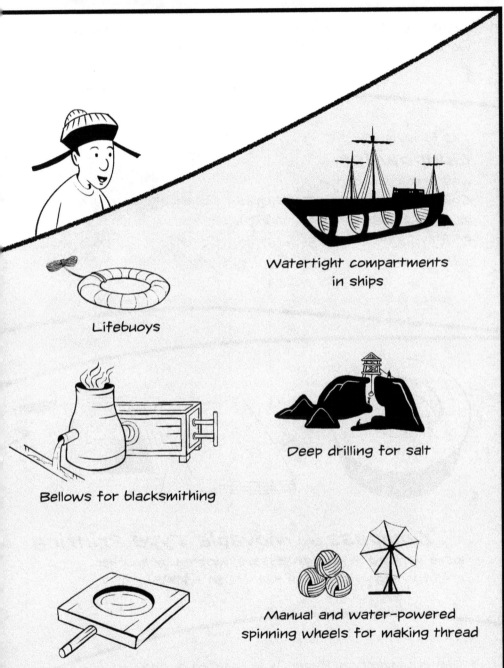

Lifebuoys

Watertight compartments in ships

Bellows for blacksmithing

Deep drilling for salt

Magnifying glass for reading

Manual and water-powered spinning wheels for making thread

Additionally, three of the Four Great Chinese Inventions were created during this period of time.*

The formula for

Gunpowder

was first recorded in *Collection of Military Techniques* by Zeng Gongliang (998 – 1078), an ally of Wang Anshi.

The **Compass** and **Movable Type Printing** were detailed in *Mengxi Essays*, written by another ally of Wang Anshi, Shen Kuo (1031 – 1095).

* The 4th invention, Paper, was created during the Han dynasty.

Along the River
at the Qingming Festival

Wang Anshi's New Policy reforms revived the country.

By the early 12th century, the Song capital of Bianjing had
become the commercial and industrial center of the empire.
Its population surpassed one million, making Bianjing
the largest city in the world at that time.

This prosperity was depicted by a Song artist in his painting
Along the River at the Qingming Festival, by far the most
famous of all Chinese paintings.

The 17-foot-long canvas captured the daily life of 814 people in Bianjing and its suburbs.

street vendor

trader

traveler

official

monk

repair shop worker

boatman

coachman

sedan bearer

Business was conducted everywhere, as people came from all over China to trade.

Many businesses opened at night.
For the first time, the Chinese had a nightlife.

Renewed struggles with the north

After a decade of reform, Emperor Shenzong felt the Song was ready to wage war once again.

Even 100 years after its founding, the Song still deals with many of the same problems faced by states during the Five Dynasties and Ten Kingdoms period!

The Xia block the Silk Road and the Liao have taken the Great Wall region. They help each other, posing a long-term threat to the nation's stability!

Send one million men to invade the Xia. We must finish them quickly before the Liao can intervene.

The 1081 invasion was the largest military operation the Song had ever undertaken.

It didn't go well.

Our troops reached the Xia capital but were unable to take it.

Then winter came. We were stuck in our summer clothing and faced shortages of food and weapons as the Xia attacked our supply lines.

The enemy has mounted a major offensive. We've lost 600,000 men!

Bad news from the frontline has woken me up in the middle of the night. I've been pacing around since dawn...

Emperor Shenzong

The depressed emperor died at age 37. Wang Anshi died shortly thereafter in 1086.

The artistic emperor

The rulers who succeeded Emperor Shenzong continued to wage war against the Xia. By the time of Emperor Huizong, the Song army had retaken a strategic mountain range region along the Song-Xia border.

Xia

Emperor Huizong
(1082 - 1135)

To finance the war, the Song issued national banknotes in 1120. This was the world's earliest paper currency.

Emperor Huizong was one of the more artistic rulers in Chinese history. He was a well-respected poet, musician, painter, and calligrapher.

His handwriting was so liked it is still used as a font on Chinese computers.

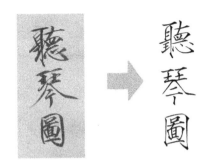

Huizong tried to make the Song spiritually superior to the Liao and Xia states.

In Taoism, the Jade Emperor is the creator and ruler of the universe.

I'm the incarnation of his eldest son. I've come to this world for the salvation of all people.

The Song will officially worship the Jade Emperor each year.

The Jade Emperor has remained a popular Chinese cultural icon till this day.

Rise of the Jurchens

Just as the Xia were about to be defeated by the Song,
the Liao dispatched a major force to help them.
The Song advance was thwarted. At the same time in 1114,
the Jurchen tribes were rising to power in northeast Asia.

The Liao used
our warriors as mercenaries.
We died for their wars for centuries!

It's time for them to pay!

Wanyan Aguda
(1068 – 1123)

Aguda started off with
less than 1,000 warriors.
Following a series of victories,
that number grew to 10,000.

In 1115, Aguda founded
the Jin dynasty (1115 – 1234).

To defeat the Liao dynasty once and for all, the Jin invited the Xia and Song to attack the Liao from three sides.

Whatever you can take from the Liao will be yours!

The Xia and Song accepted the alliance. In 1125, the Liao collapsed in chaos.

In 10 years, the Jin went from a tiny tribe to a powerful state.

We've taken most of the Liao land. The surrendered Liao army is now under our command.

Last days of the Northern Song

In 1127, the Jin led a surprise attack on the Song capital and captured the entire Song government, including Huizong and his family. The Song dynasty in northern China, known as the Northern Song, ended.

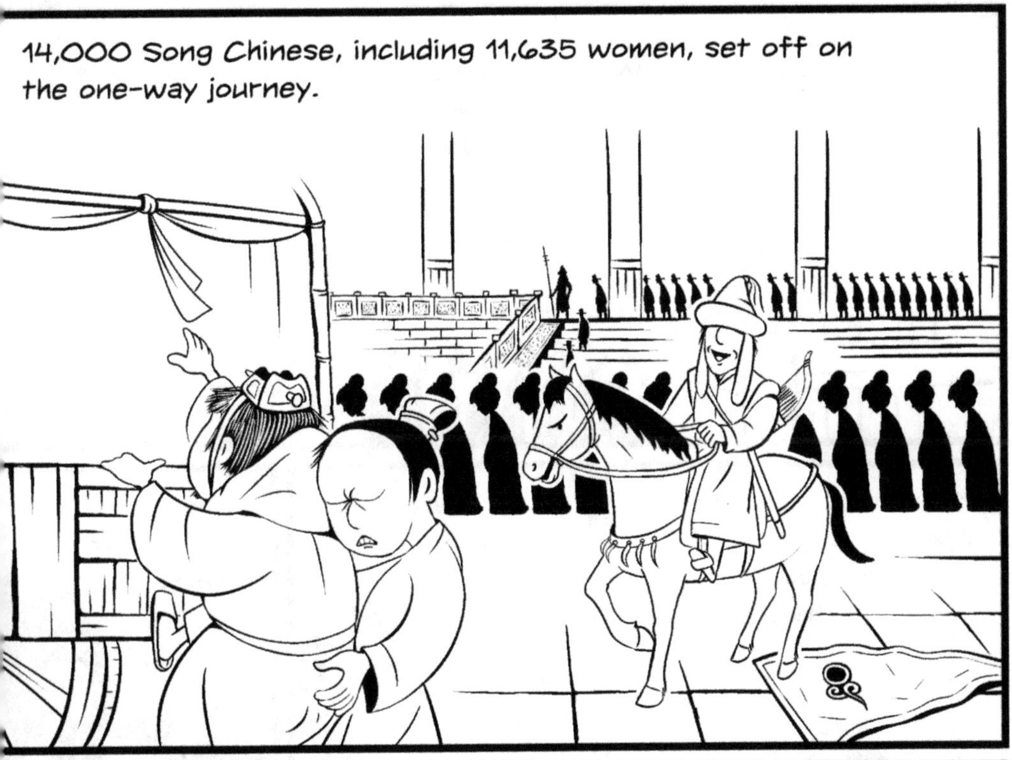
14,000 Song Chinese, including 11,635 women, set off on the one-way journey.

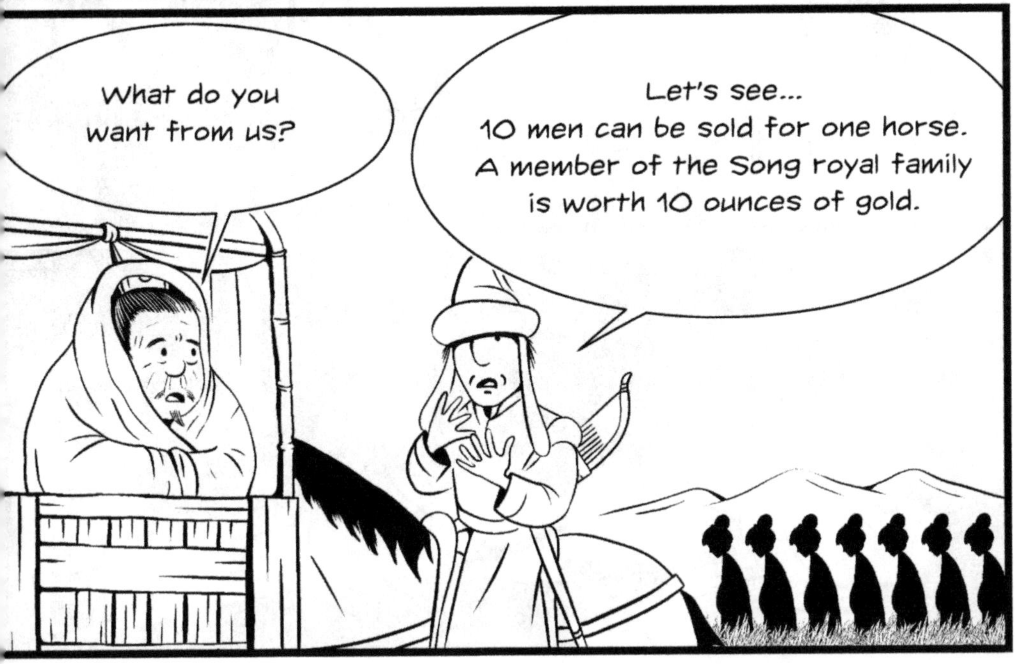
What do you want from us?
Let's see... 10 men can be sold for one horse. A member of the Song royal family is worth 10 ounces of gold.

We also have 21 of Huizong's daughters. The oldest is 28 and the youngest is 4.

After they arrived in Jin territory, a lucky few Song Chinese served in the Jin palace.

Many were sold as slaves.

Most were tortured to death.

Emperor Huizong, once a Son of Heaven, died a broken man in a foreign land.

Some historians believe that the tragic ending of the Northern Song and subsequent raids from the north helped create the custom of Chinese foot binding.

To prevent their girls from being taken away by the raiders, parents bound their feet.

When the girls grew older, their feet would be deformed and remain small.

To the nomads, women with bound feet were useless.

What?! They can't ride horses?!

Mom, my feet hurt.

I know it's painful, but it'll keep you safe.

One very famous novel written in the 14th century gives insight into the fall of the Northern Song.

Water Margin*

水浒传

This classic told stories of 108 outlaws. These warriors banded together to form a rebel army, but later surrendered to the government and joined campaigns to resist foreign invaders and suppress rebellions.

* Sometimes known as *The Outlaws of the Marsh*

Shifting south

Only one son of Emperor Huizong escaped capture.
His name was Zhao Gou.

Zhao Gou
(1107 – 1187)

In June 1127, Zhao Gou declared himself emperor,
establishing the Southern Song dynasty (1127 – 1279).

Following Zhao, one million refugees, including 20,000 officials
and 400,000 soldiers, fled south.

The Southern Song didn't have a reliable army to defend itself.

Two army commanders took over the court and forced me to abdicate the throne.

After other generals rescued me, they in turn took control. I no longer have any power.

Many generals insist on fighting the Jin. In reality, they use the war as an excuse to hold on to power.

Some fake reports to boost their rankings, hide defeats, and cheat the state for funding.

Widespread riots further weakened
the Southern Song defenses.

There are several groups
of bandits in each province.
Each group has at least
100,000 people.

I have no choice but to
beg for peace with the Jin.

If the semi-independent
generals drag on the war,
we'll not only fail to recover the north,
but also lose the south.

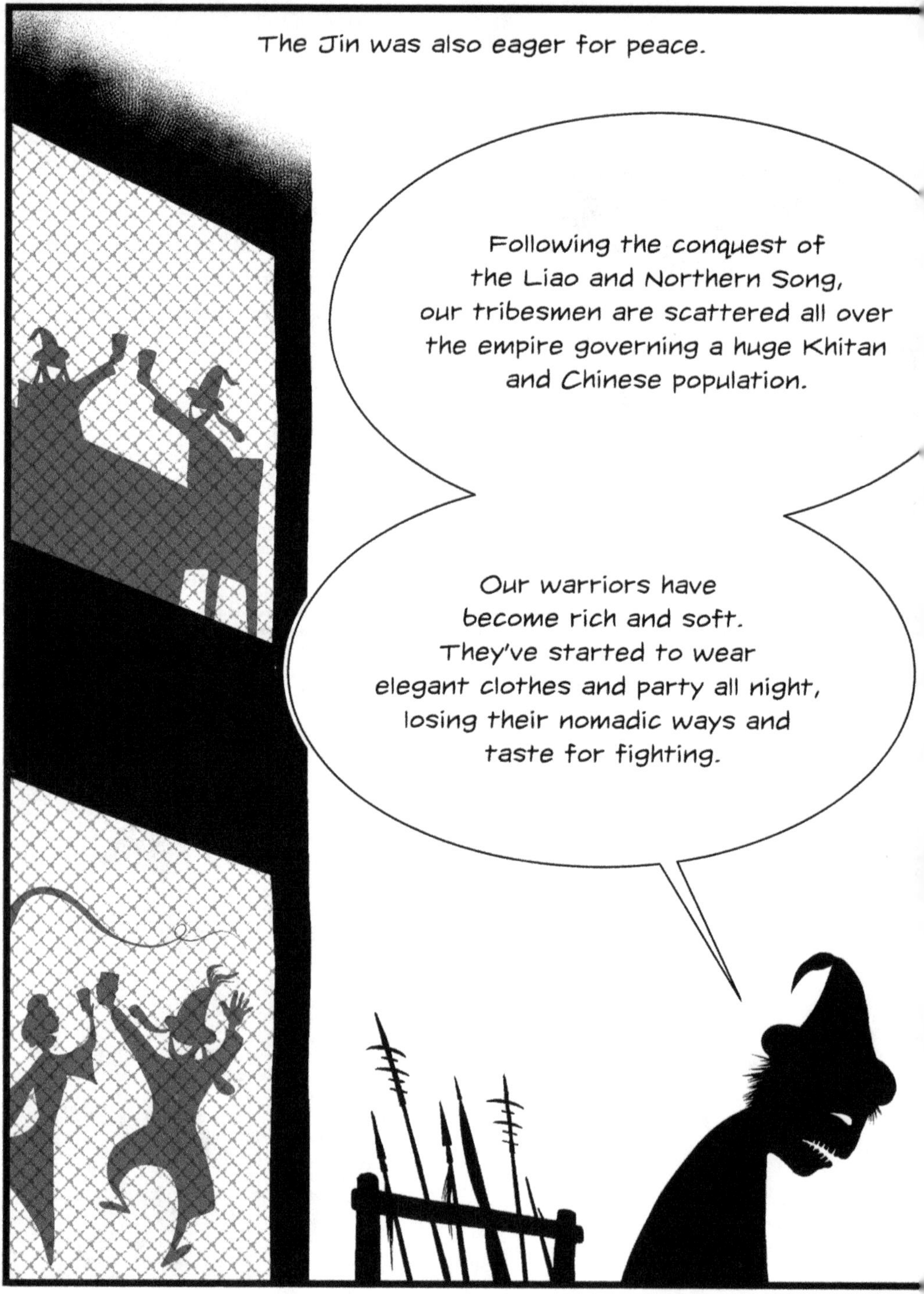
The Jin was also eager for peace.
Following the conquest of the Liao and Northern Song, our tribesmen are scattered all over the empire governing a huge Khitan and Chinese population.
Our warriors have become rich and soft. They've started to wear elegant clothes and party all night, losing their nomadic ways and taste for fighting.

In 1141, the Jin and Southern Song signed the Treaty of Shaoxing. The treaty made 30 million northern Chinese, or 30% of China's population, subjects of the Jin dynasty.

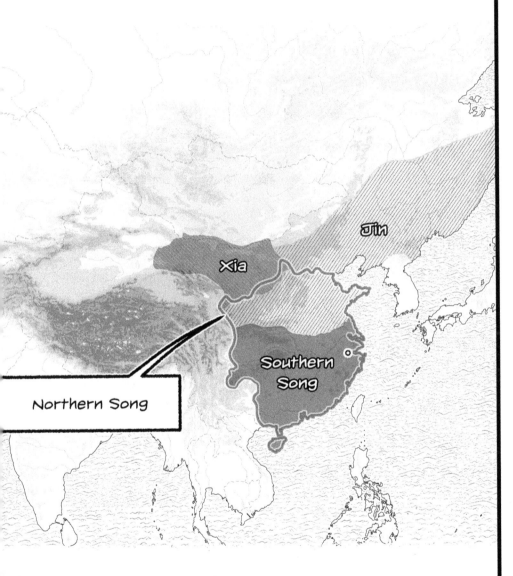

Jin

Xia

Southern Song

Northern Song

◎ Capital Lin'an (Hangzhou)

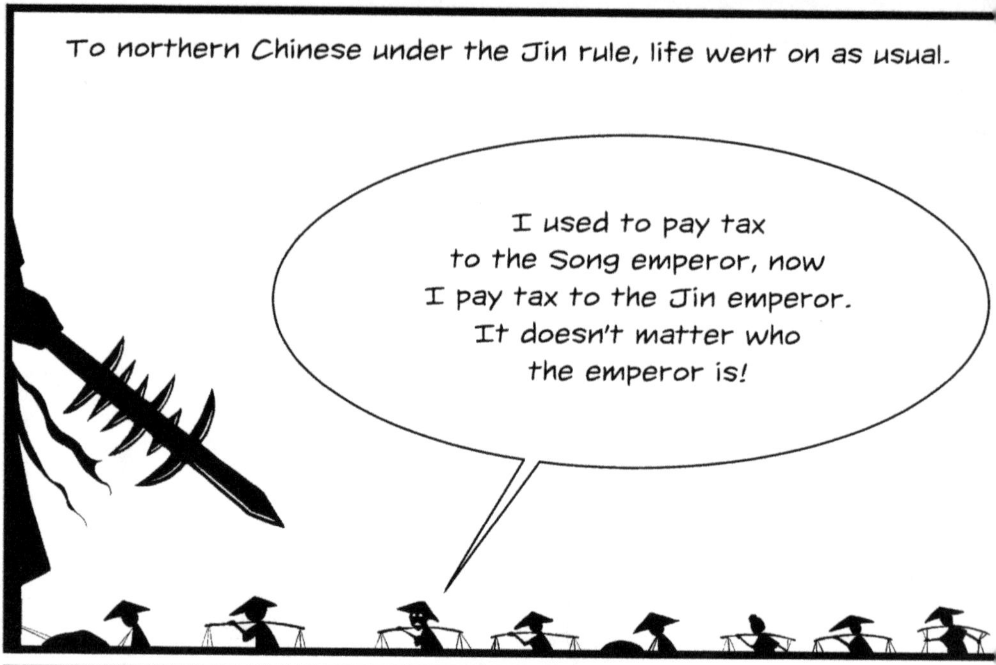
To northern Chinese under the Jin rule, life went on as usual.
I used to pay tax to the Song emperor, now I pay tax to the Jin emperor. It doesn't matter who the emperor is!

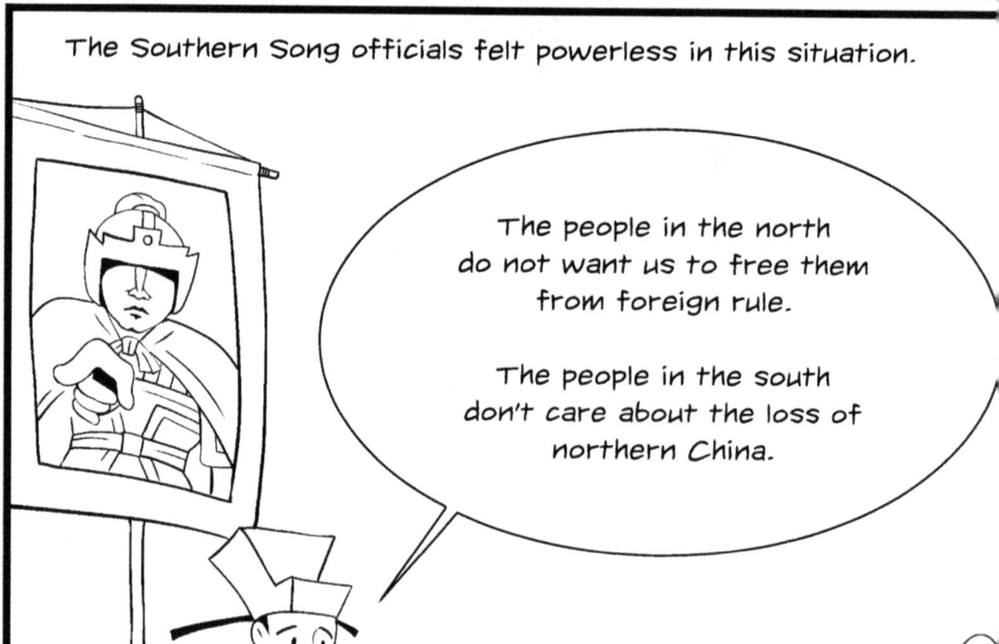
The Southern Song officials felt powerless in this situation.
The people in the north do not want us to free them from foreign rule.
The people in the south don't care about the loss of northern China.

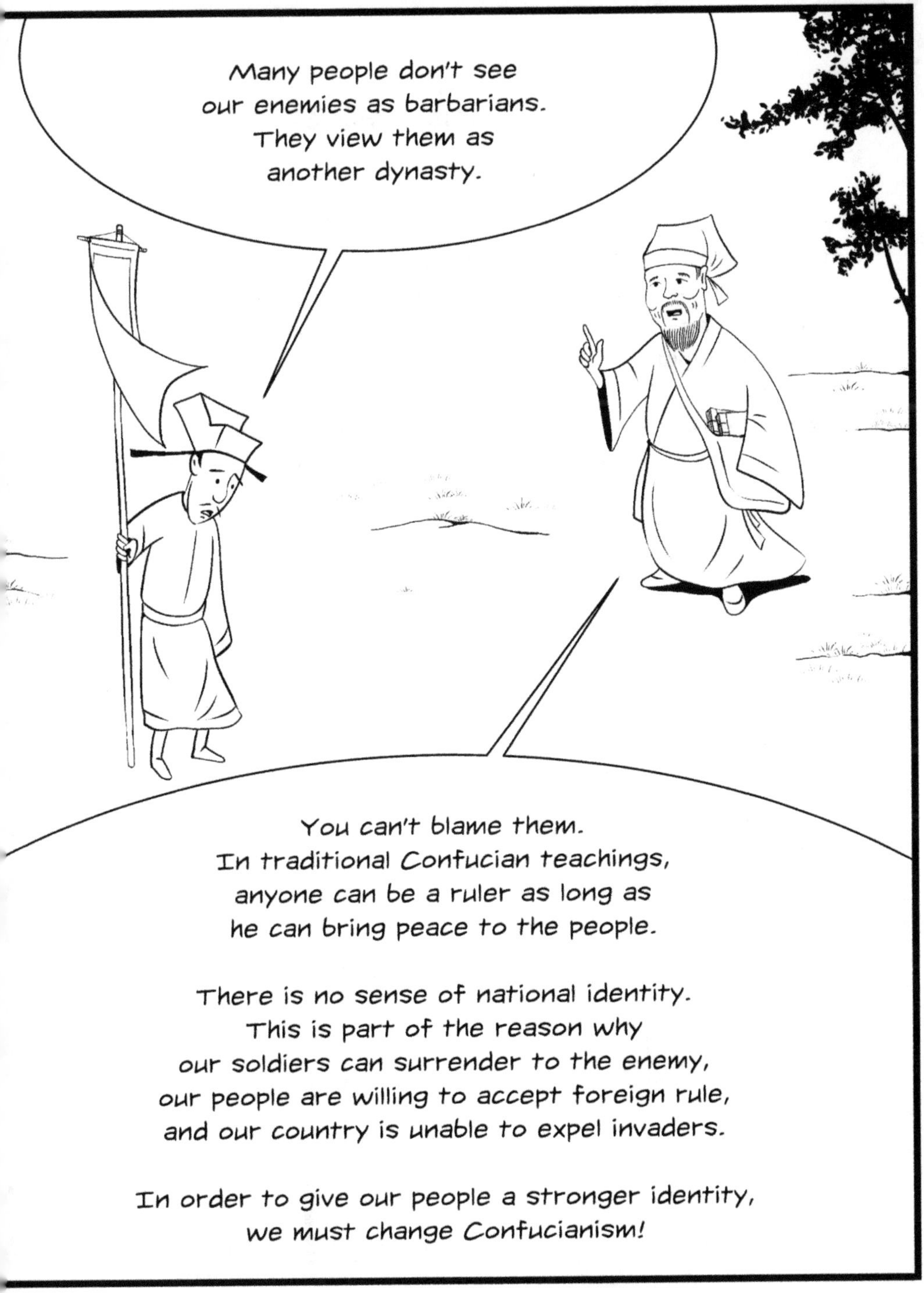
Many people don't see our enemies as barbarians. They view them as another dynasty.
You can't blame them. In traditional Confucian teachings, anyone can be a ruler as long as he can bring peace to the people.

There is no sense of national identity. This is part of the reason why our soldiers can surrender to the enemy, our people are willing to accept foreign rule, and our country is unable to expel invaders.

In order to give our people a stronger identity, we must change Confucianism!

Neo-Confucian movement

Over the course of the Song, Chinese thinkers sought to reform Confucianism. In the process they created entirely new schools of thought. These schools were collectively known as Neo-Confucianism, an ideology that would dominate Chinese thought for 800 years.

One of the most influential Neo-Confucians was a Southern Song scholar-official, Zhu Xi (1130 – 1200).

I went to school at 5,
passed the imperial examination at 19,
and held several government positions for 10 years.
I've also spent 50 years writing books
and teaching in private schools.

Zhu Xi integrated previous Chinese views of the universe into one system.

Everything has Li (principle)
and Qi (vital force).

For example, people first discover
the principle of boat building, and then
they find the right materials, a vital force
with specific form, to make a boat.

理
Principle

气
Vital force

The source of different principles and
vital forces is Taiji, or the supreme principle,
which has existed since the beginning of the universe.

To understand the abstract supreme principle,
we start with understanding the principles
of physical things, including ourselves.

Zhu Xi's major contribution to Neo-Confucianism was in reforming the traditional Confucian curricula that had been used for more than 1,000 years.

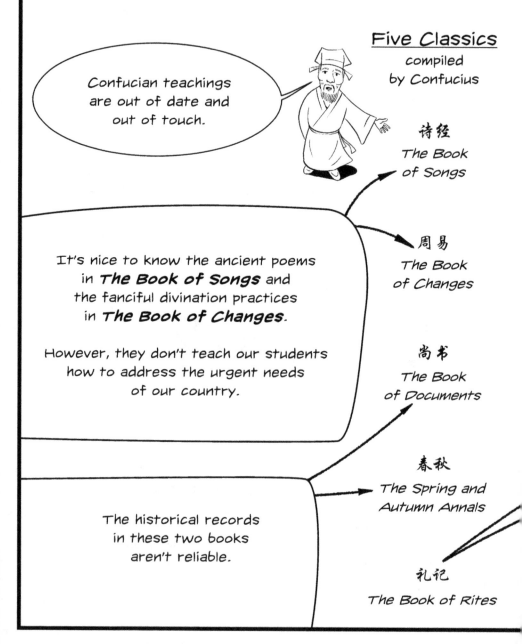

Confucian teachings are out of date and out of touch.

Five Classics
compiled by Confucius

诗经
The Book of Songs

周易
The Book of Changes

It's nice to know the ancient poems in *The Book of Songs* and the fanciful divination practices in *The Book of Changes*.

However, they don't teach our students how to address the urgent needs of our country.

尚书
The Book of Documents

春秋
The Spring and Autumn Annals

The historical records in these two books aren't reliable.

礼记
The Book of Rites

Only **The Book of Rites**
has some practical use since it focuses on
a standard of conduct. I picked two out of
its 49 chapters that students should study.

My new curricula will teach students
why it's important to study and
what kind of men they should be.

Four Books

compiled by Zhu Xi

大学
The Great Learning

中庸
The Doctrine of the Mean

论语
"The Analects" of Confucius

孟子
Mencius

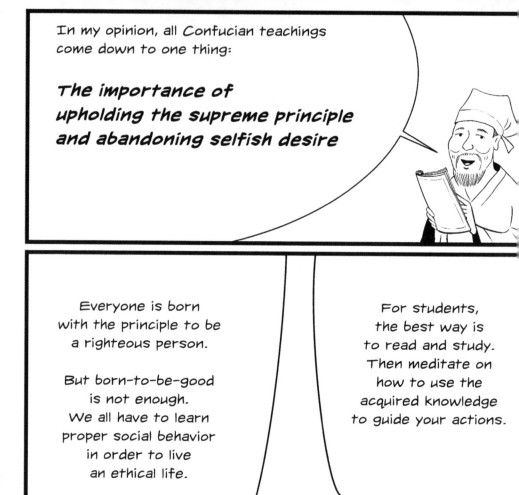

In my opinion, all Confucian teachings come down to one thing:

The importance of upholding the supreme principle and abandoning selfish desire

Everyone is born with the principle to be a righteous person.

But born-to-be-good is not enough. We all have to learn proper social behavior in order to live an ethical life.

For students, the best way is to read and study. Then meditate on how to use the acquired knowledge to guide your actions.

In Zhu Xi's time, official schools only taught the Five Classics and all students had to study them in order to pass imperial exams.

I set up a private school to teach the Four Books. I initially had 10 students.

Inspired by Zhu Xi, other local officials and prominent scholars opened similar private academies. Doing so laid the foundation for the Four Books to become the bedrock of Confucian education till 1905.

Zhu Xi was one of the most productive scholars in Chinese history. His existing works have a total of 13.5 million characters.
These books cover such topics as history, philosophy, government, education, art, ritual, and etiquette.

Thanks to his efforts, the family took its place at the center of Confucian teachings for the first time.

Previous books about rites focused on state ceremonies. I wrote this as a guidebook for families.

The Family Rituals
家礼

Daily etiquette

Dress code

Weddings

Funerals

Ancestor worship

Zhu Xi's followers simplified his ideas so that even children could understand.

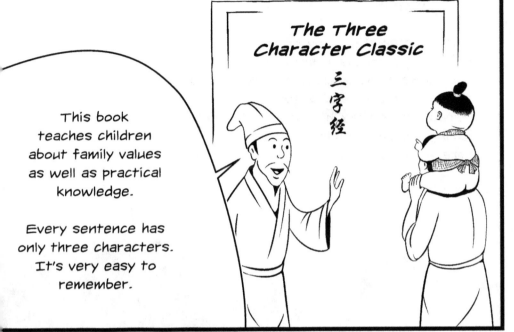

The Three Character Classic

三字经

This book teaches children about family values as well as practical knowledge.

Every sentence has only three characters. It's very easy to remember.

Today, every Chinese person can recite the opening lines of **The Three Character Classic** by heart.

人之初 — People at birth

性本善 — Are naturally good

性相近 — Their natures are similar

习相远 — Their habits make them different

Zhu Xi and his fellow Neo-Confucians took
this updated version of Confucian education
and pushed it to new heights.

Their systematic study of the world,
reformed curricula in schools,
and books made available to commoners
thanks to the spread of printing
helped define the Chinese as "Chinese"
during a period in which invasion by
foreign powers was constantly a threat.

In 1194, Zhu Xi became an imperial advisor.
But he soon found himself caught up in
a showdown between two rival factions.

We must fight the Jin to retake the Central Plain of China!

The Song doesn't have enough cavalry or supplies to wage a war against barbarians on horseback.

Han Tuozhou (1152 – 1207), a military officer from a consort clan

Zhao Ruyu (1140 – 1196), a councilor and member of the imperial clan

We should first strengthen our position domestically with Neo-Confucianism, then we can deal with external threats.

Emperor Ningzong (1168 – 1224)

The emperor wanted war and supported the army's position.

You spend every day studying your supreme principle. This makes your backbone weak.

Banish Zhao Ruyu, Zhu Xi, and 59 other Neo-Confucians! Ban Neo-Confucian teachings!

Zhu Xi only lasted 40 days in the court.
He died in disgrace several years later in 1200.

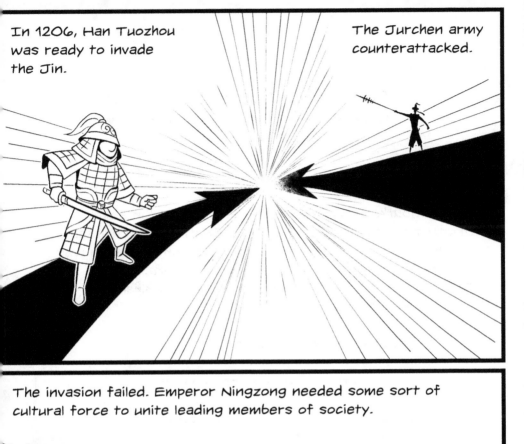

In 1206, Han Tuozhou was ready to invade the Jin.

The Jurchen army counterattacked.

The invasion failed. Emperor Ningzong needed some sort of cultural force to unite leading members of society.

Restore Neo-Confucianism. All schools must use the curricula compiled by Zhu Xi.

THE MONGOL EMPIRE

1206 – 1368

As the Southern Song and Jin were engaged in a war
of attrition, a nomadic tribe in the Central Asian plateau
united into a single confederation. This confederation was
later to become known as the Mongol Empire.
In 1206, their leader took the title Genghis Khan,
or the Lord of Lords.

Over the course of the 13th century,
the Mongols swept through Asia and Eastern Europe,
establishing the largest land empire in history.

China was both the starting point and climax
of the Mongol's conquest.

The Mongolian ethnic roots
were from the Shiwei (a Khitan tribe),
the Mohe (the Jurchens' ancestors), and the Turks.

The gigantic Mongol empire begins with the story of one man – Temujin (1162 – 1227).

Born into a tribal chieftain's family, Temujin grew up in a toxic, unstable environment.

Temujin saw his father murdered.

His wife was kidnapped.

Temujin fought more than 100 tribes to unite the Mongols under his rule.

There is no greater joy than killing one's enemies, seizing all of their belongings, and taking their wives and daughters.

When Temujin proclaimed himself Genghis Khan, he made his first target the Jin dynasty.

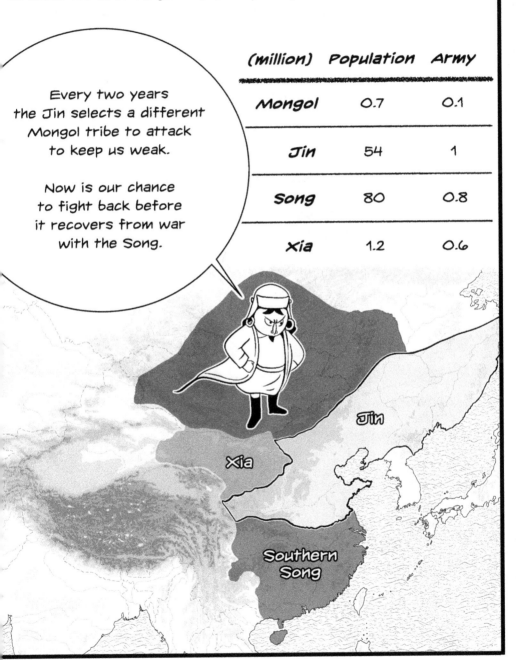

Every two years the Jin selects a different Mongol tribe to attack to keep us weak.

Now is our chance to fight back before it recovers from war with the Song.

(million)	Population	Army
Mongol	0.7	0.1
Jin	54	1
Song	80	0.8
Xia	1.2	0.6

Mongol world conquest begins

In 1211, 90,000 Mongol cavalry rode out to invade the Jin, leaving only 2,000 to guard their home base.

We have the smallest army and population in this region. If we are to beat the Jin, we need the help of the Xia and Song.

If we want them to follow us to war, we need a decisive victory. After all everyone wants to be on the winner's side.

Mongol capital Karakorum

Jin Central Capital (Beijing)

In August, the Mongols arrived at the Jin defensive line, 120 miles north of the Jin Capital.

On the day of battle, Genghis Khan led his men to the mountain pass.

We'll break through the enemy's frontline defenses to attack their command center and supply camps.

Arrows and rocks poured down on them.

The Mongols just kept coming.

But suddenly, chaos broke out in the Jin army.

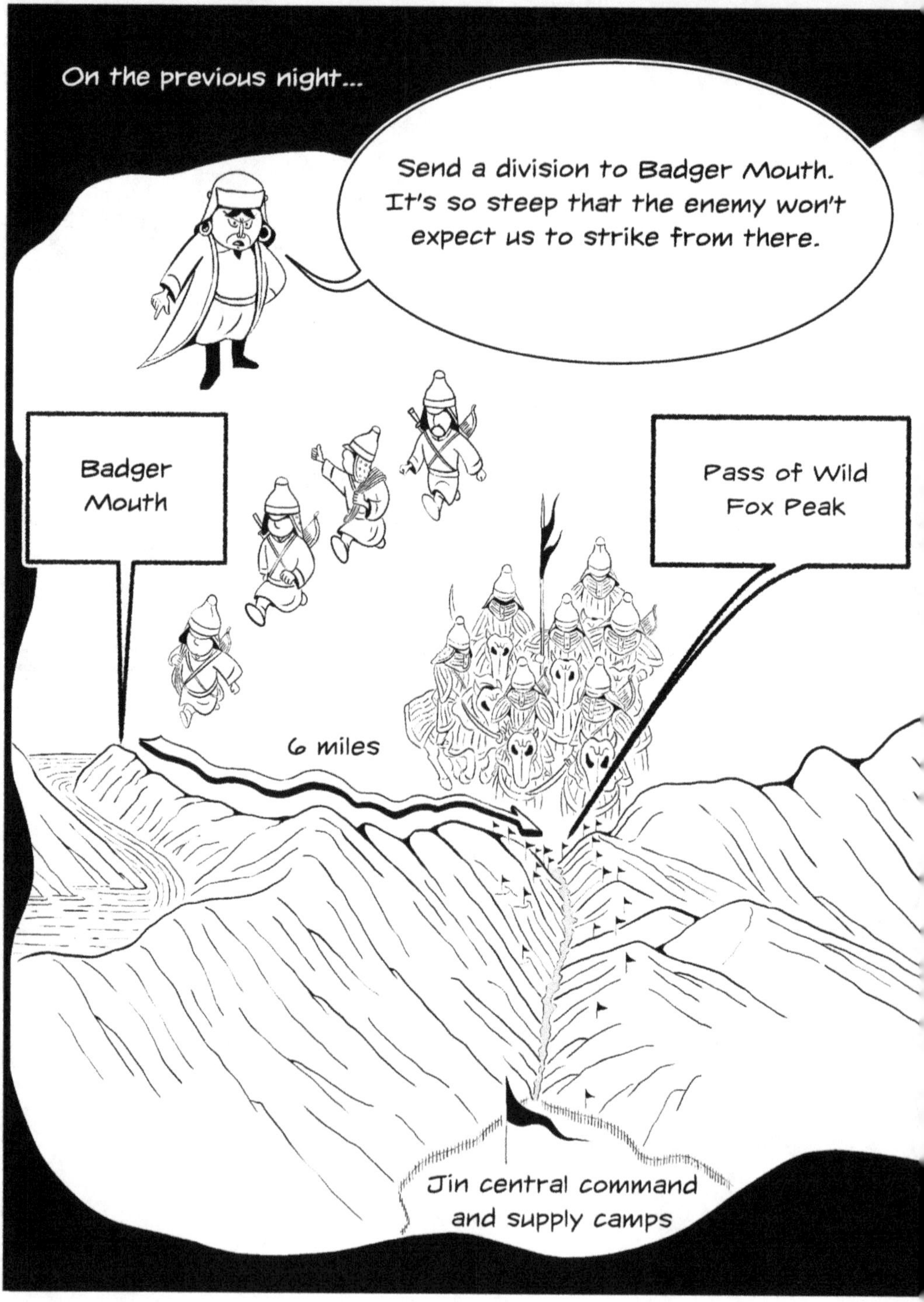
On the previous night...
Send a division to Badger Mouth. It's so steep that the enemy won't expect us to strike from there.
Badger Mouth
Pass of Wild Fox Peak
6 miles
Jin central command and supply camps

While the attack at the mountain pass attracted the attention of the Jin units, the Mongol division secretly climbed the slopes...

...seized the guard towers...

...and moved to attack the Jin from behind.

The surprise attack took the pressure off the Mongol cavalry. They were able to break through the mountain pass and destroy the Jin central command and their supplies.
Terrified Jin soldiers fled.

This campaign, known as the Battle of Badger Mouth,
was one of the bloodiest battles in history.
The Jin lost nearly 400,000 troops.

The Mongols considered it the most important victory
in consolidating their Empire.

The Jin dynasty soon crumbled after this defeat.

The Western Xia agreed to a military alliance with the Mongols and began a decade-long war with the Jin.

The Jin attacked the Southern Song, hoping to recoup some of their territorial losses.

A few years after the Battle of Badger Mouth, the Jin was isolated and fighting a war on three fronts.

The Mongols, on the other hand, had secured regional supremacy and soon began looking farther abroad for new territory to conquer.

Genghis Khan alternated his focus between conquests in southern China and westward expeditions into Central Asia. Each victory brought him more land, money, and slaves.

Destruction of the Xia and Jin

In 1224, Genghis Khan was alarmed by a new development. The Western Xia had begun openly resisting his rule.

The Mongols are working us to death!

The Xia, Jin, and Song should fight against the Mongols, not each other!

Genghis Khan answered this defiance with overwhelming force. In 1227, his army destroyed the Xia capital.

The victory cost him his life.

Ögedei Khan continued the Mongol conquest of China.
Soon it was clear that the Jin couldn't hold on much longer.

The Song attacked the Jin from the south, hoping to
recapture its long-lost land in northern China.

In 1234, the last Jurchen defense collapsed,
bringing the Jin dynasty to an end.

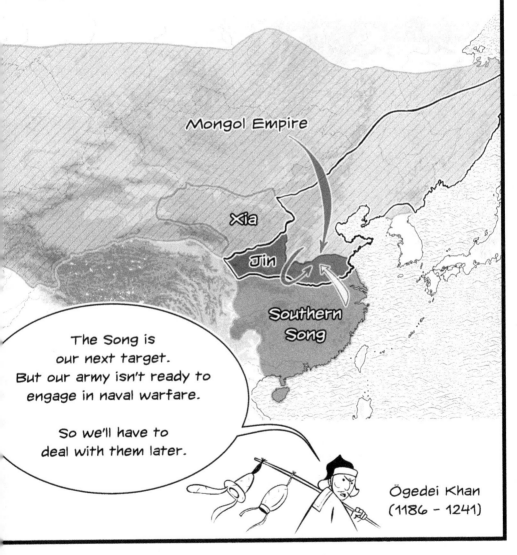

Mongol Empire

Xia

Jin

Southern
Song

The Song is
our next target.
But our army isn't ready to
engage in naval warfare.

So we'll have to
deal with them later.

Ögedei Khan
(1186 – 1241)

The Southern Song before Mongol conquest

With the Mongol advance temporarily halted, the Southern Song wasted no time in building up its military strength.

Besides a huge infantry, we have a navy with 52,000 marines and 22 fleets. Our paddle-wheel ships are armed with catapults that can launch fire bombs.

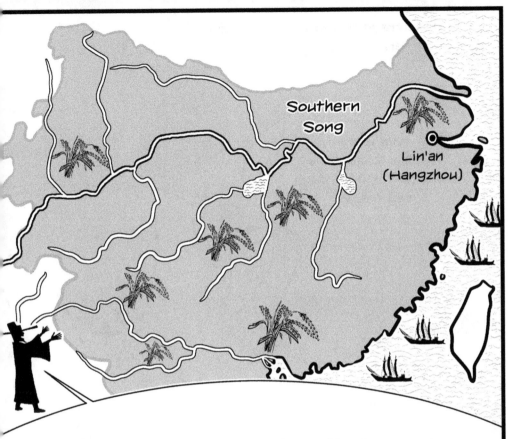

We are also very wealthy and can afford to spend a lot on our defenses. Look what we have:

 The majority of rice-producing regions in China

 A vast inland shipping network

 A long coastline with seaports suitable for international trade

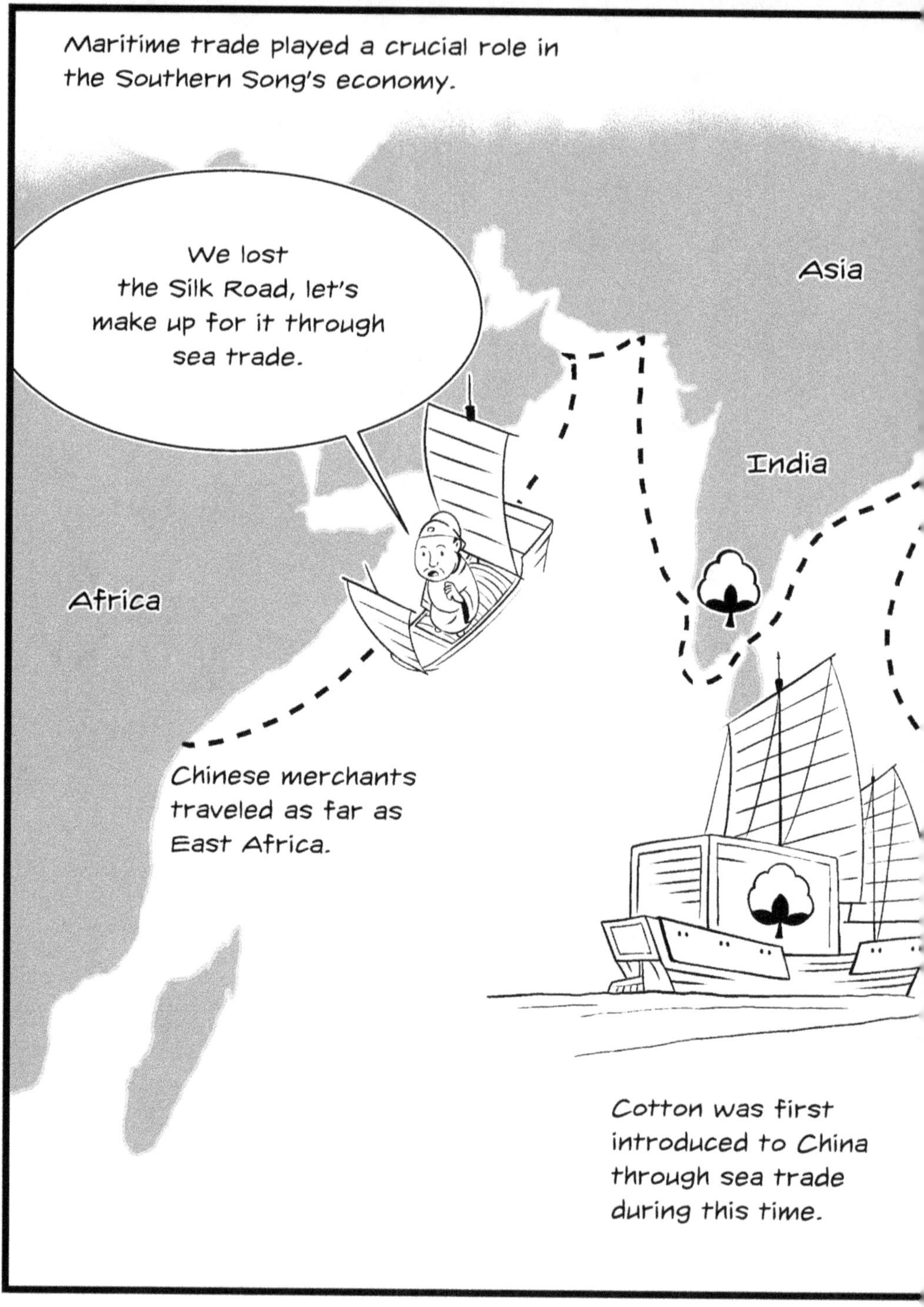
Maritime trade played a crucial role in the Southern Song's economy.
We lost the Silk Road, let's make up for it through sea trade.
Asia
India
Africa
Chinese merchants traveled as far as East Africa.
Cotton was first introduced to China through sea trade during this time.

Quanzhou became the largest port in the world. It was later known as the starting point of the Maritime Silk Road.

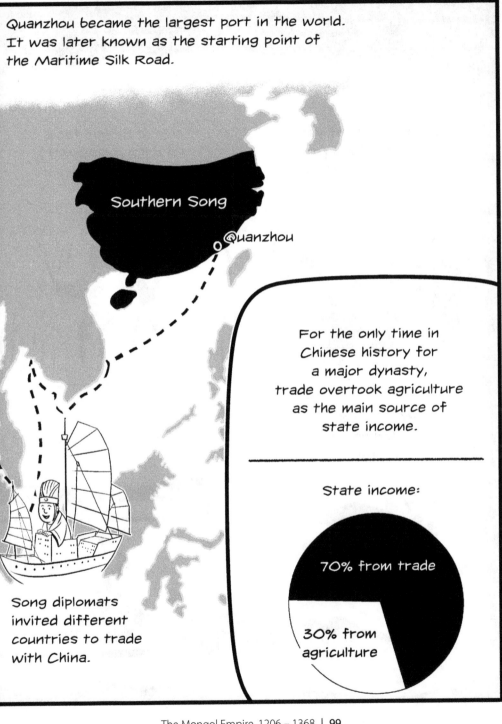

Southern Song

○ Quanzhou

For the only time in Chinese history for a major dynasty, trade overtook agriculture as the main source of state income.

State income:

70% from trade

30% from agriculture

Song diplomats invited different countries to trade with China.

Trade greatly impacted the lives of farmers.

For thousands of years before the Song, rural life had remained unchanged.

We grow our food, and pay taxes with parts of our harvest.

We buy salt and clothes once a year.

For the most part, we're stuck in one place.

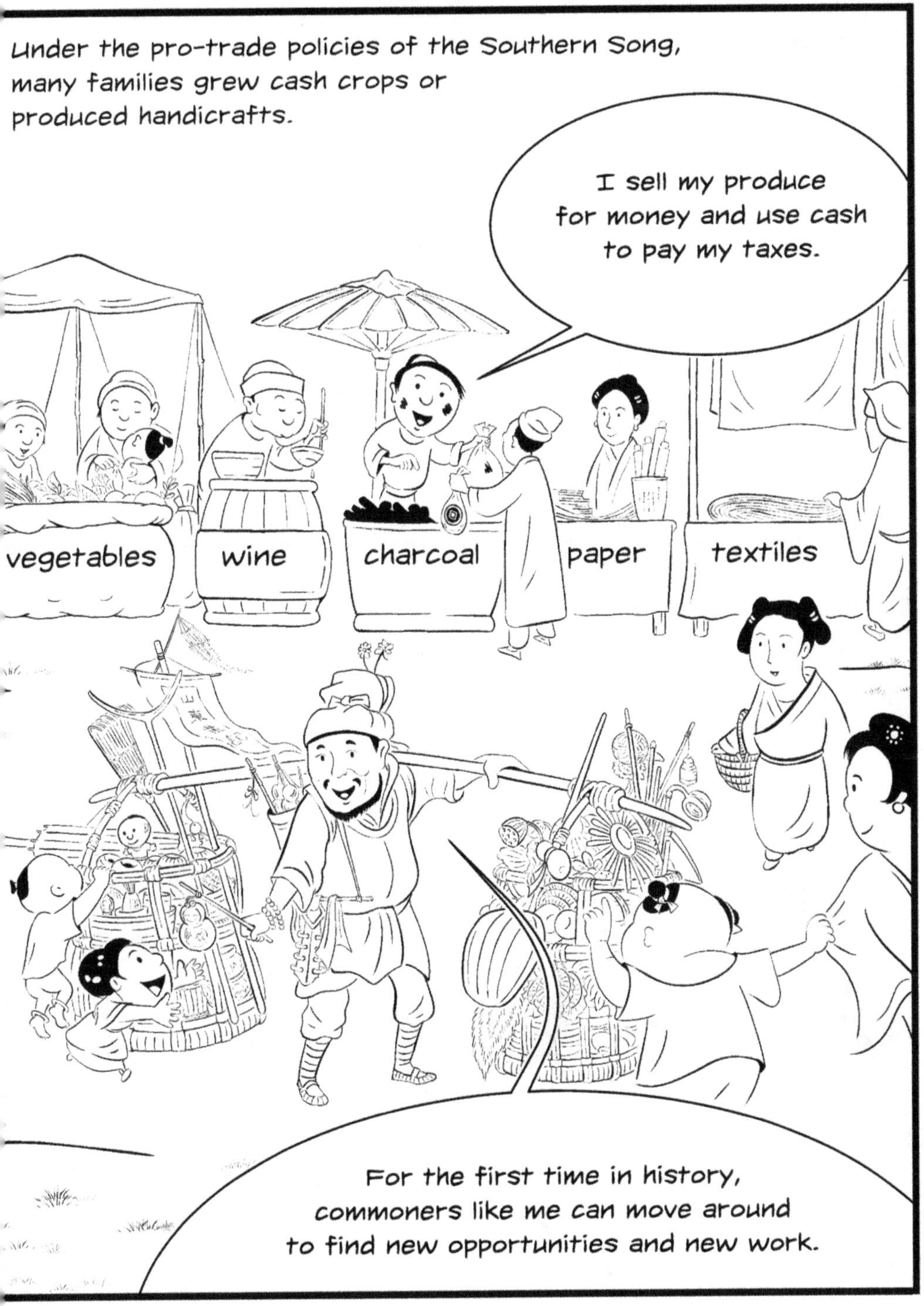

Under the pro-trade policies of the Southern Song, many families grew cash crops or produced handicrafts.
I sell my produce for money and use cash to pay my taxes.
vegetables
wine
charcoal
paper
textiles
For the first time in history, commoners like me can move around to find new opportunities and new work.

Commercial expansion led to rapid growth of cities.

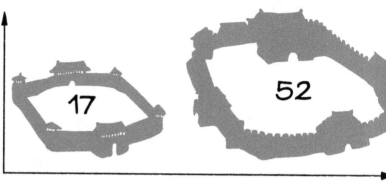

Cities with population above 100,000

17 — Tang dynasty

52 — Song dynasty

Merchants came from many different parts of the country. For those who had connections, there were quick and easy ways to make a fortune. Many others started small businesses.

Ruling elites looked down on merchants.

These people buy and sell things made by others. Everything they do is for profit. They contribute little to the state.

To protect their interests, merchants organized themselves into guilds. These associations dealt with the government in matters such as taxation, law enforcement, and public obligations.

In large cities, many things that used to be reserved for royalty became available to commoners. Ordinary people could learn calligraphy, painting, poetry, essays, opera, music, and dance.

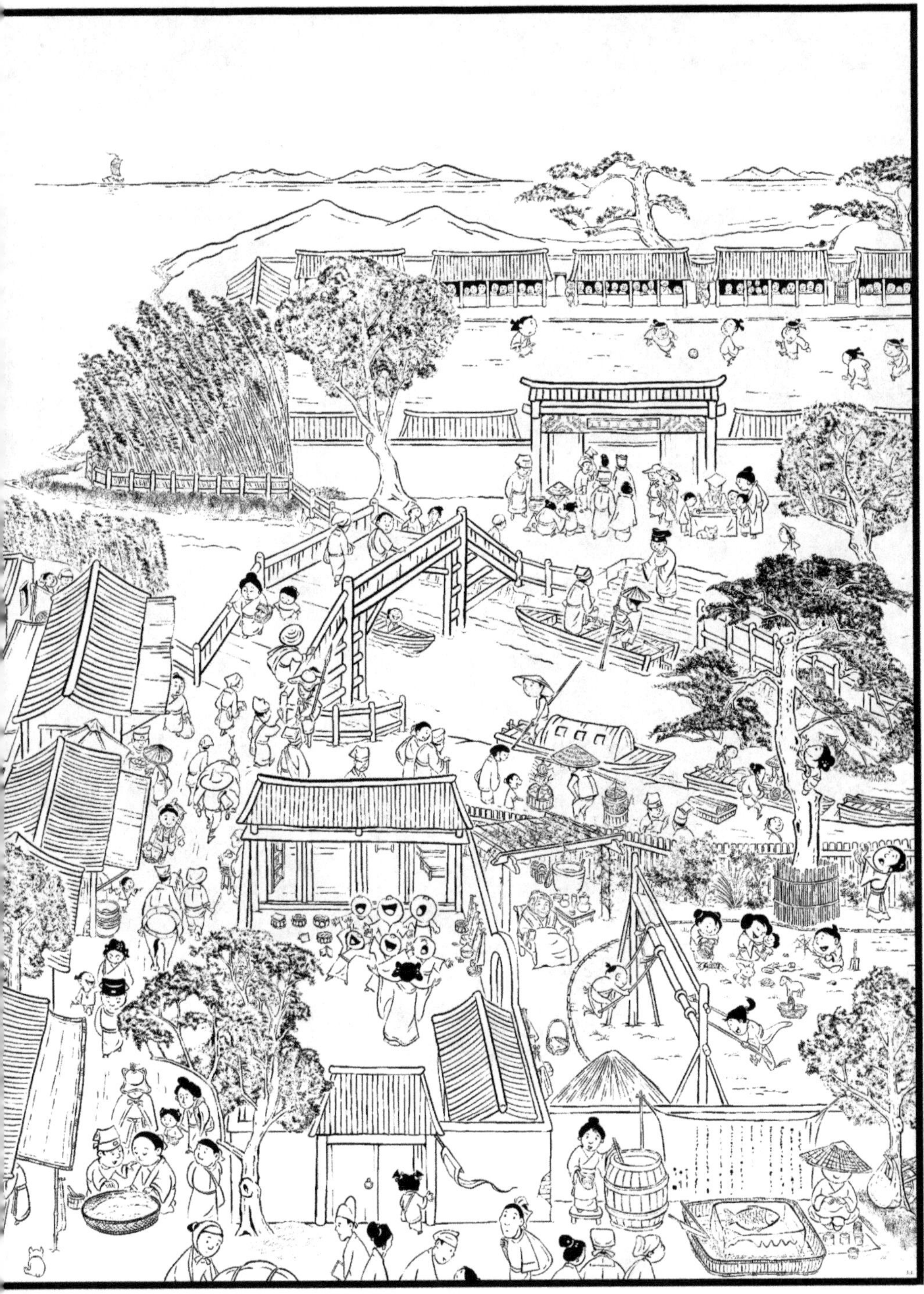

The Mongols are back!

Before urbanization and commerce could bring permanent change to China, the Mongols were back.

Two decades had passed since their initial conflict with the Southern Song. This time, they were much stronger.

With siege weapons captured from the Xia and Jin, the Mongols were able to defeat the Turkic tribes in Central Asia and Islamic states in the Middle East.

Using conquered soldiers as auxiliaries, the Mongols swept through Russia, Poland, and Hungary. Their armies reached as far as Austria and northeast Italy.

Asia

Europe

Mongol Empire

Southern Song

Africa

When the Mongol invasion began again in 1257, the Southern Song faced a very different enemy from the one they had fought years earlier. This time the Mongols controlled the resources of around 30 nations.

A little Fishing Town

The Mongol ruler personally led the invasion.
After winning many battles, his army came upon a tiny fortress
called Fishing Town .

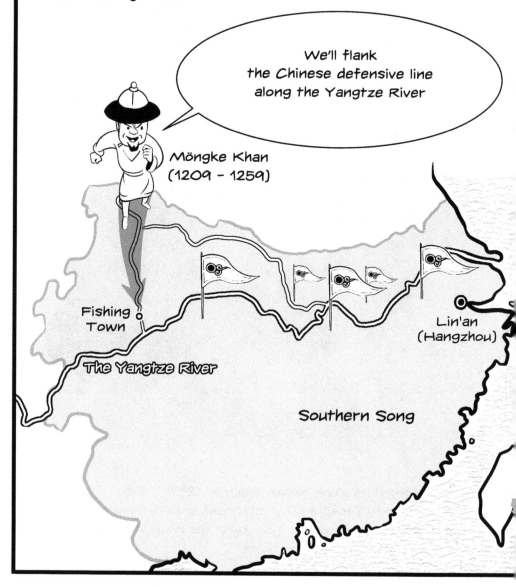

We'll flank
the Chinese defensive line
along the Yangtze River

Möngke Khan
(1209 – 1259)

Fishing
Town

Lin'an
(Hangzhou)

The Yangtze River

Southern Song

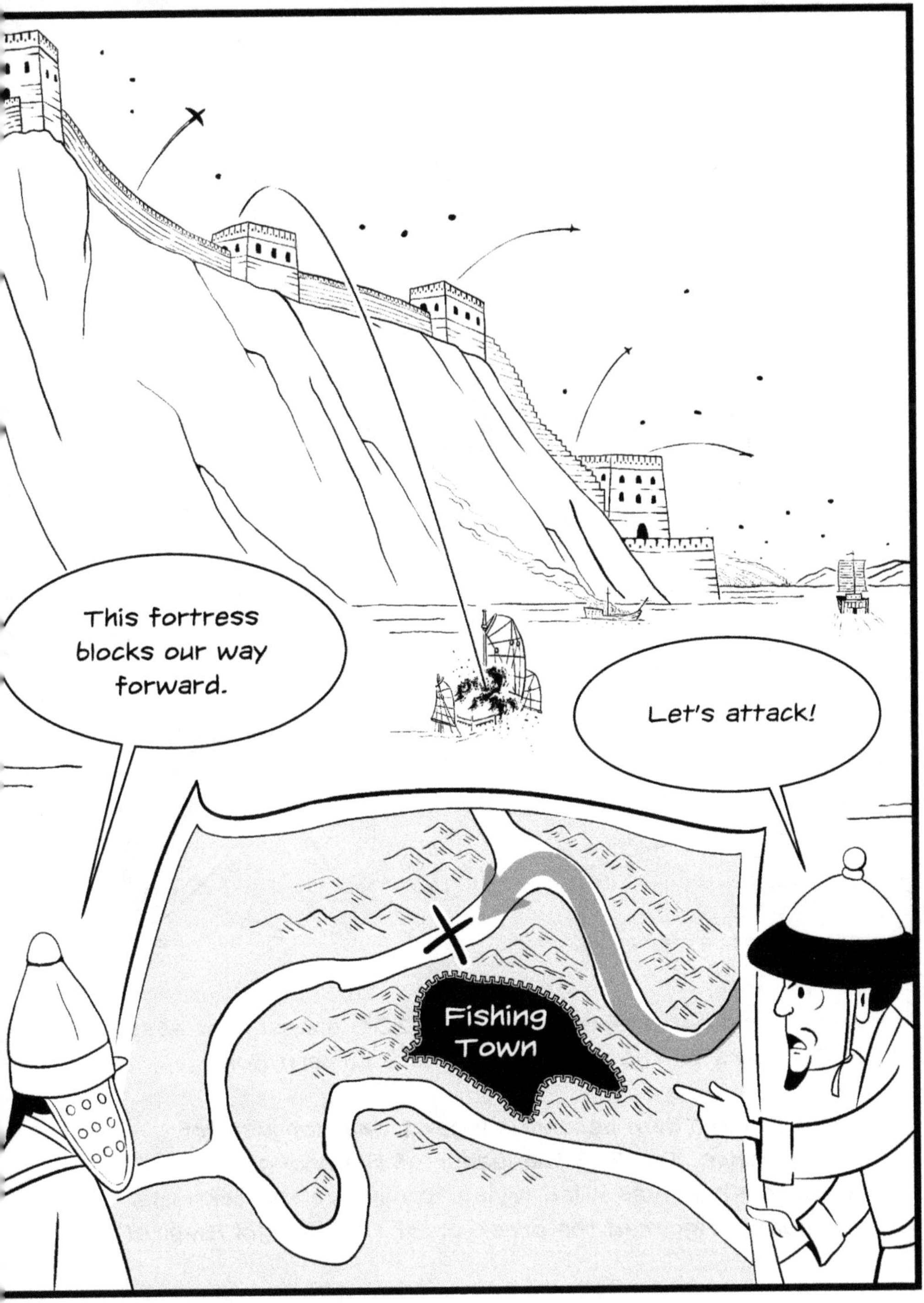
This fortress blocks our way forward.
Let's attack!
Fishing Town

The little town held out against that first assault.

And it held out against more than 200 subsequent assaults in 36 years till the very end of the Southern Song.

The Fishing Town became a legend, and not just for its resilience. In 1259 the leader of the Mongols, Möngke Khan, was killed trying to capture the fortress. His death triggered the break-up of the Mongol Empire!

The Mongol Empire is split

After Möngke Khan's death, his youngest brother asked all Mongol leaders to put their worldwide conquests on hold and return to the capital.

Respecting the wishes of Möngke, we'll hold a meeting to elect our next leader.

The new Khan will take Eastern Asia. The other princes will command subordinate states in Central Asia, the Middle East, and Eastern Europe.

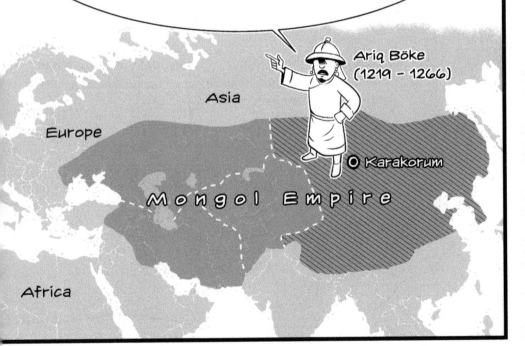

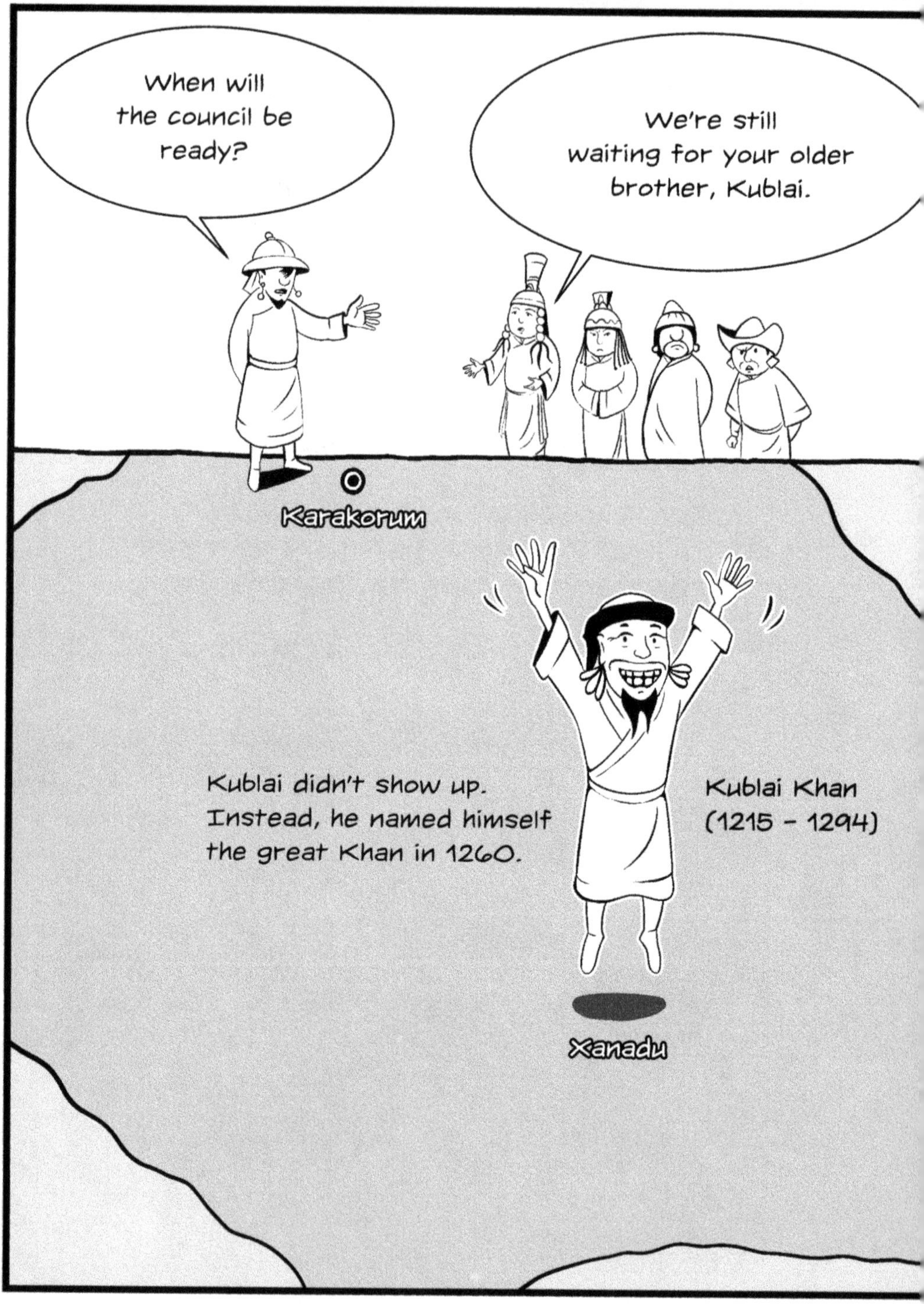
When will the council be ready?
We're still waiting for your older brother, Kublai.
Karakorum
Kublai didn't show up. Instead, he named himself the great Khan in 1260.
Kublai Khan (1215 - 1294)
Xanadu

A civil war soon broke out, dividing the Mongol Empire into four independent realms with individual Khans.

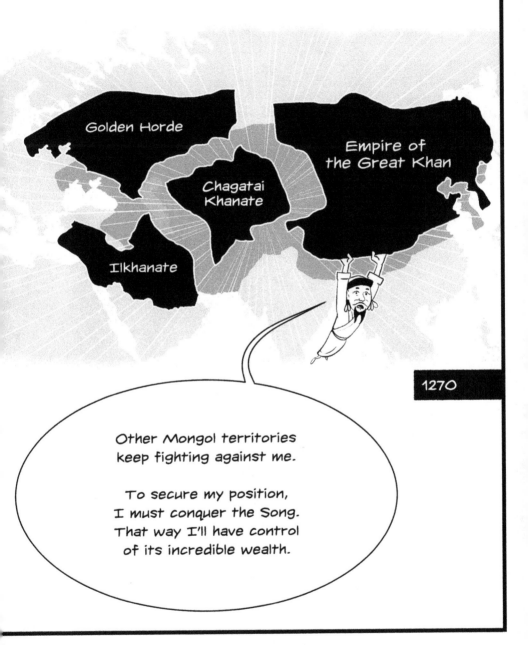

Golden Horde

Chagatai Khanate

Empire of the Great Khan

Ilkhanate

1270

Other Mongol territories keep fighting against me.

To secure my position, I must conquer the Song. That way I'll have control of its incredible wealth.

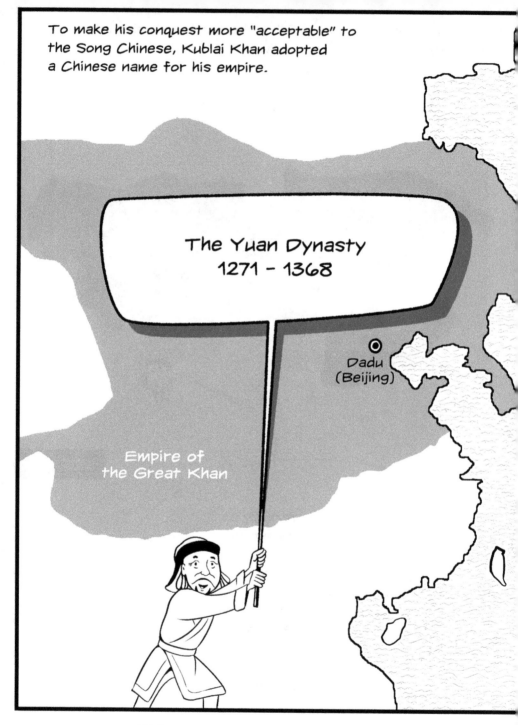

To make his conquest more "acceptable" to the Song Chinese, Kublai Khan adopted a Chinese name for his empire.

The Yuan Dynasty
1271 – 1368

Dadu
(Beijing)

Empire of
the Great Khan

Battle of Xiangyang

Kublai Khan saw the city of Xiangyang as the most important part of his China campaign.

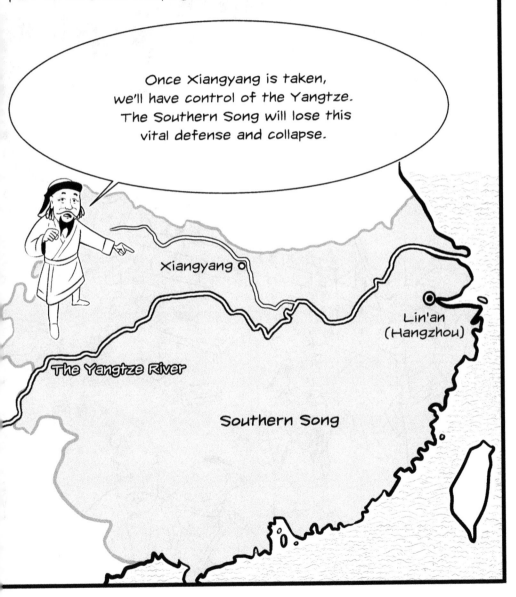

Once Xiangyang is taken, we'll have control of the Yangtze. The Southern Song will lose this vital defense and collapse.

Xiangyang

Lin'an (Hangzhou)

The Yangtze River

Southern Song

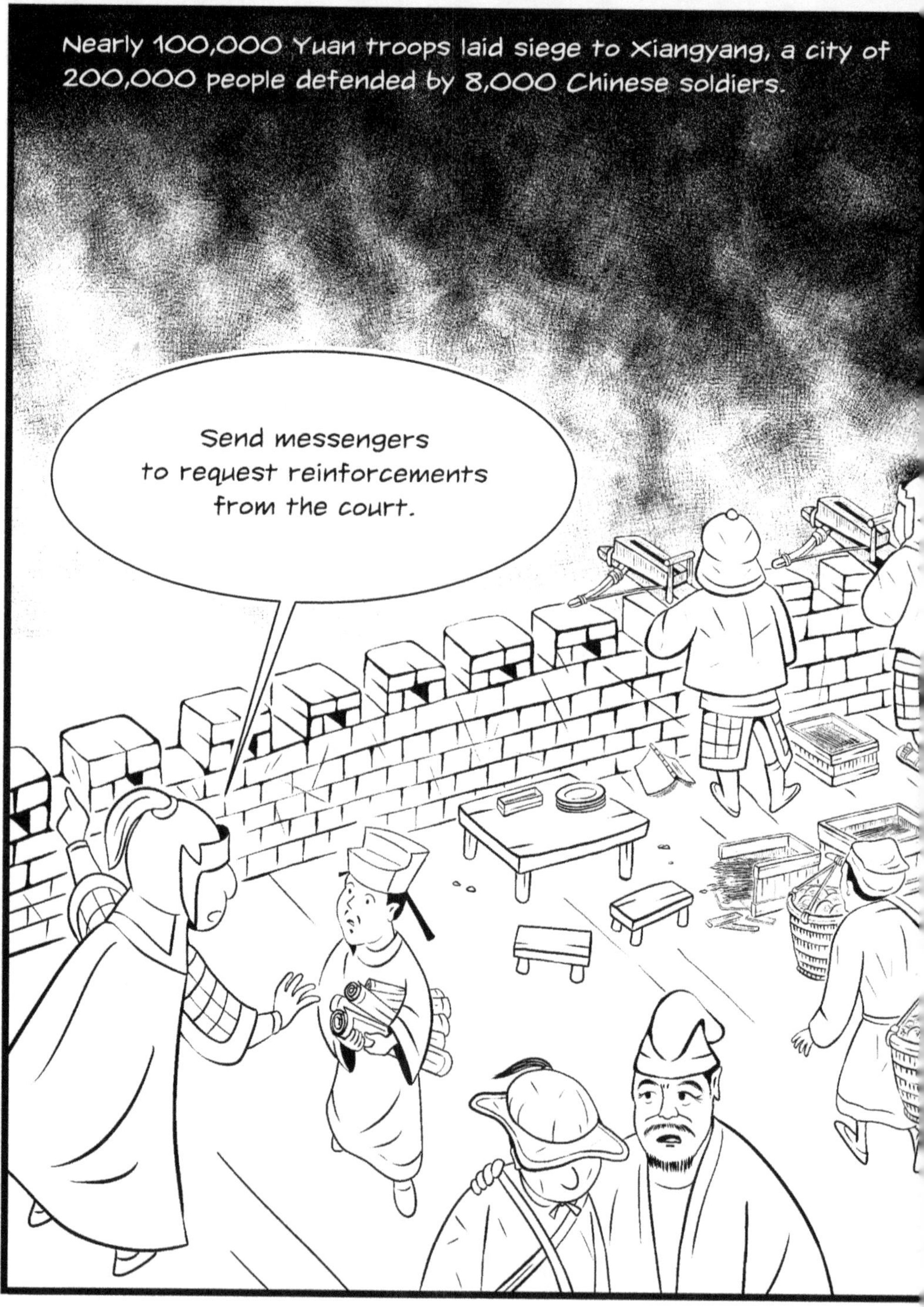
Nearly 100,000 Yuan troops laid siege to Xiangyang, a city of 200,000 people defended by 8,000 Chinese soldiers.
Send messengers to request reinforcements from the court.

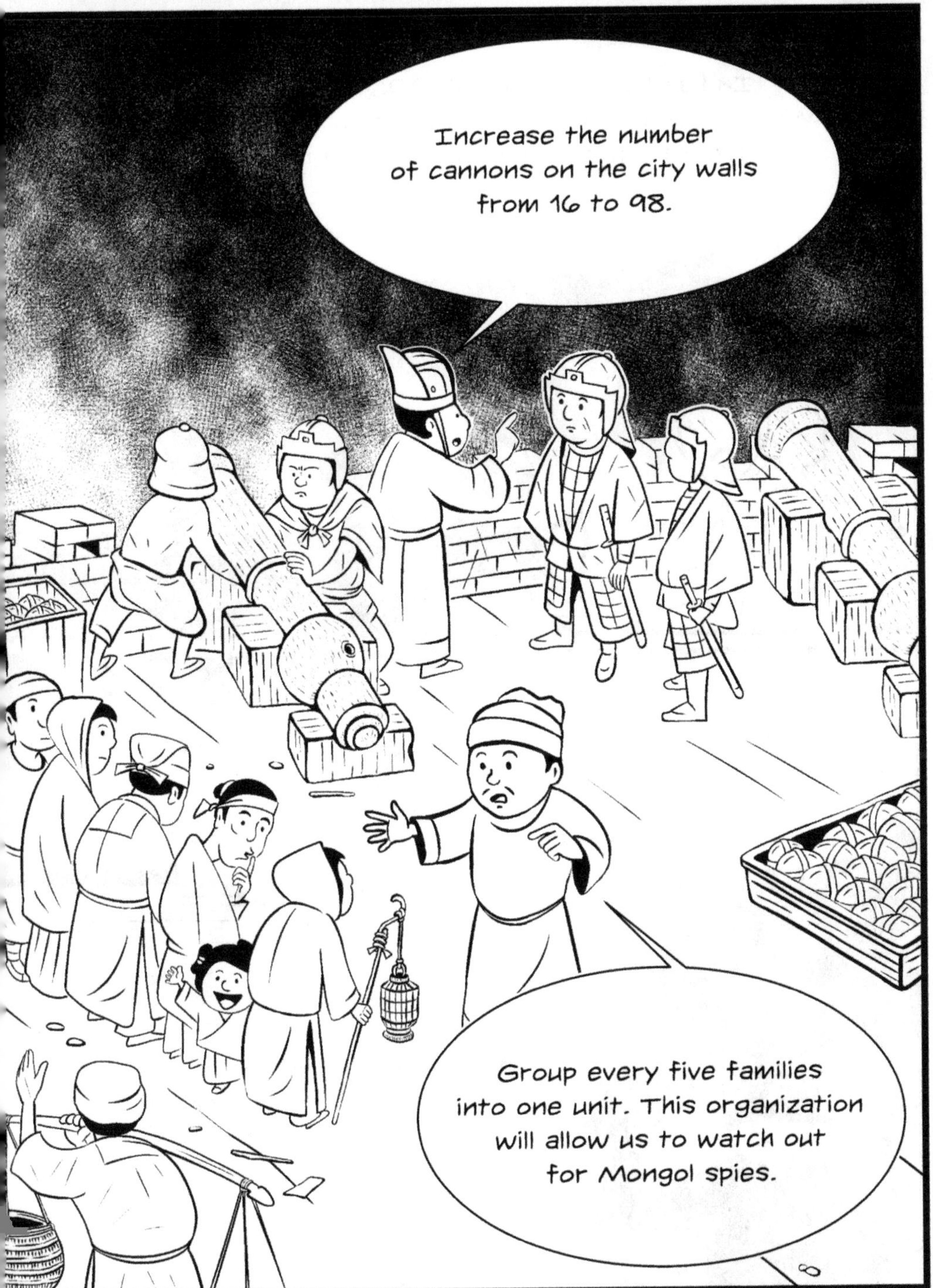
Increase the number of cannons on the city walls from 16 to 98.
Group every five families into one unit. This organization will allow us to watch out for Mongol spies.

In battle, we need 100,000 arrows each day.
With supplies running low, our special units will carry out
night raids to take arrows from the Mongols.

There is
a problem!

Most people in the surrounding area
moved into the city for safety,
leaving thousands of dogs behind.

Barking dogs will reveal our position.

Can't you use bamboo cages to trap them?

That way you can bring back arrows as well as extra food.

As the siege entered its fifth year, the Song defenders had fewer and fewer supplies with each passing day.
The Mongols have cut off the last land route into our city. Now their navy is trying to block our river supply lines.
What is that?

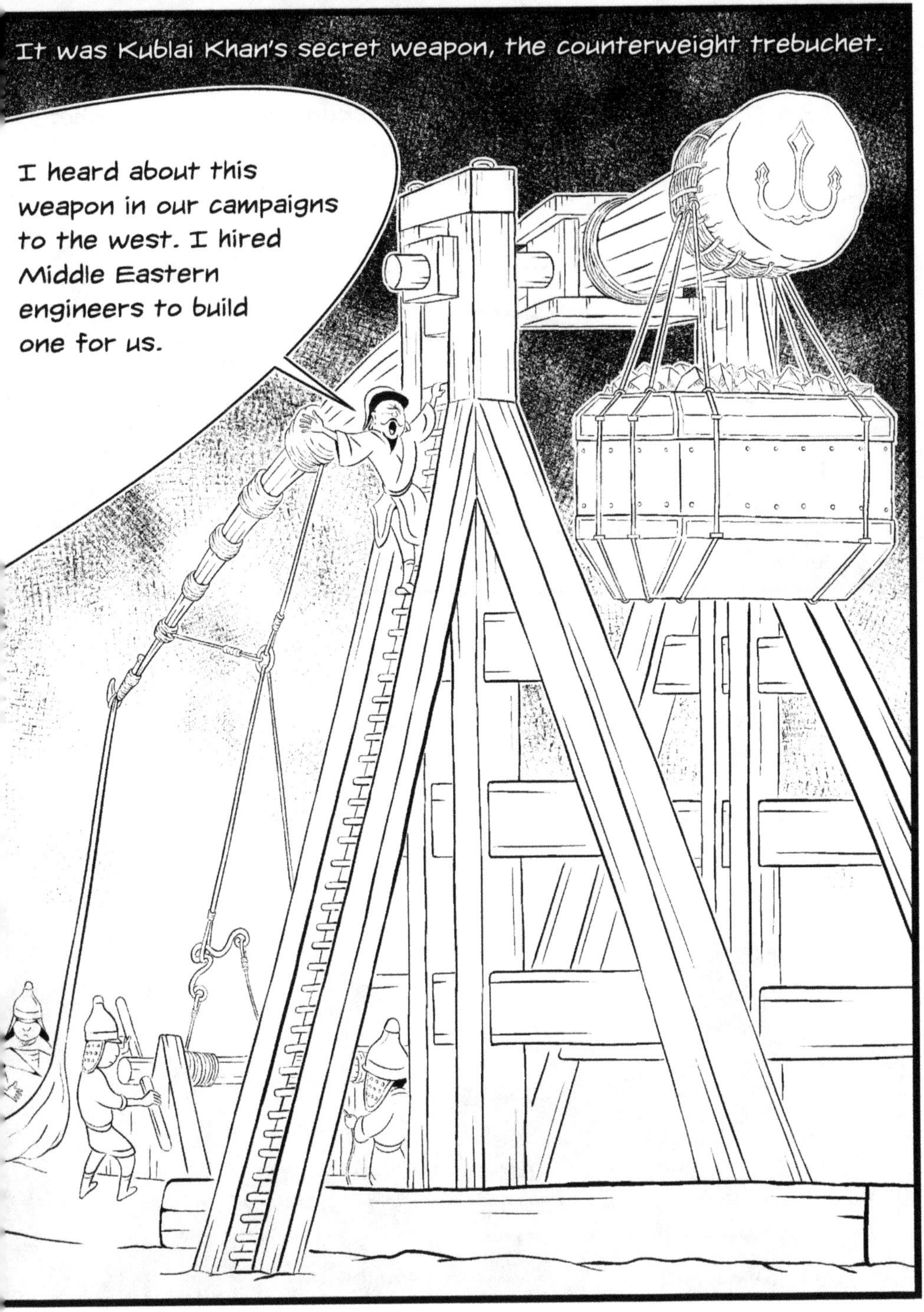

It was Kublai Khan's secret weapon, the counterweight trebuchet.
I heard about this weapon in our campaigns to the west. I hired Middle Eastern engineers to build one for us.

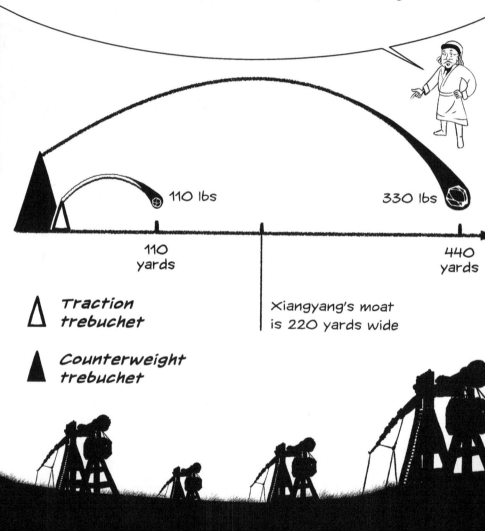

The Chinese have only seen traction trebuchets that are pulled by a group of men using ropes. My counterweight trebuchet will surprise them with its strength and range.

110 lbs

330 lbs

110 yards

440 yards

△ Traction trebuchet

▲ Counterweight trebuchet

Xiangyang's moat is 220 yards wide

By 1273, the Mongols had built 20 of these machines, capable of pulverizing city walls into dust. The Xiangyang defenses were destroyed and the city taken.

In 1276, the Yuan army entered the capital Lin'an and captured the Southern Song emperor.

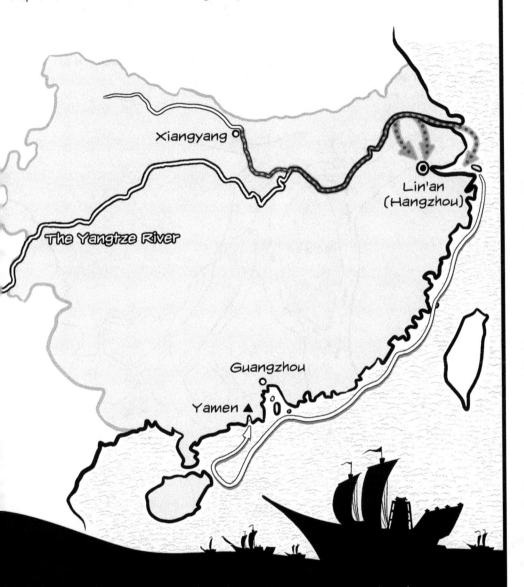

Xiangyang

Lin'an
(Hangzhou)

The Yangtze River

Guangzhou

Yamen ▲

The surviving Song loyalists put a little prince on the throne, gathering an army as they retreated south.

Last stand of the Song Chinese

In 1279, the remaining Song resistance of 200,000 men and women took refuge in a fleet of 1,000 ships.
The Yuan navy found them at Yamen.

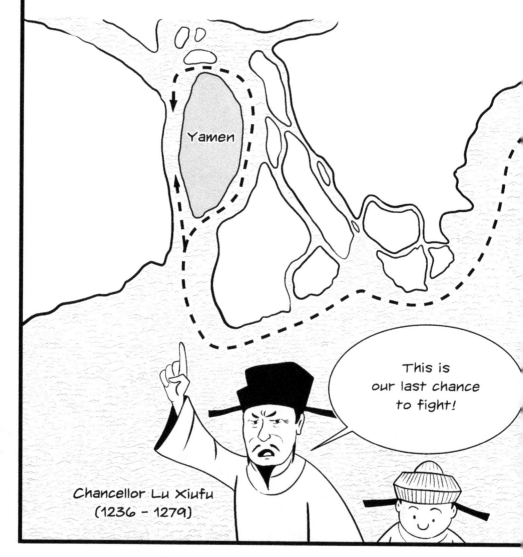

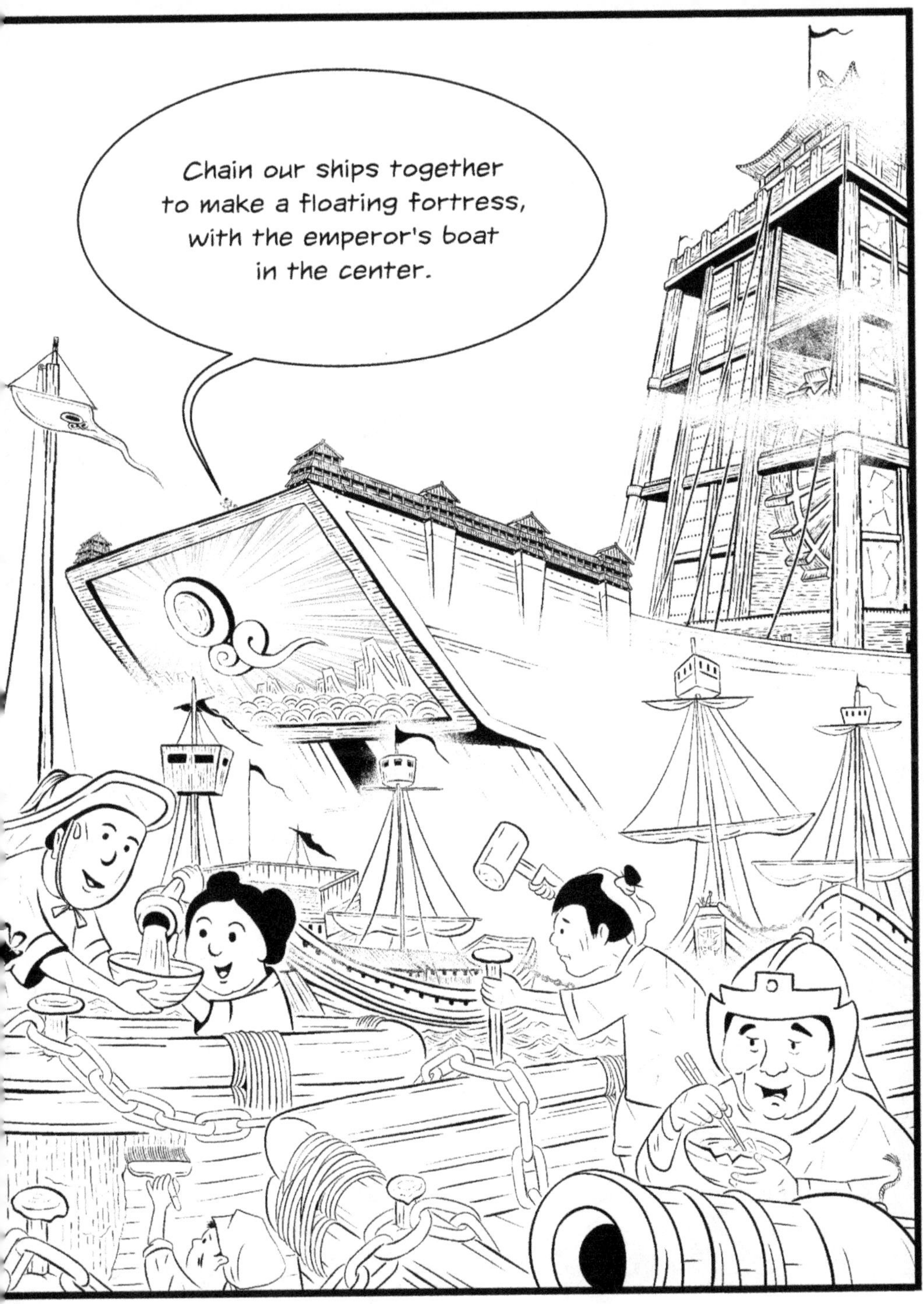
Chain our ships together to make a floating fortress, with the emperor's boat in the center.

On March 19, 1279, the main assault was launched.

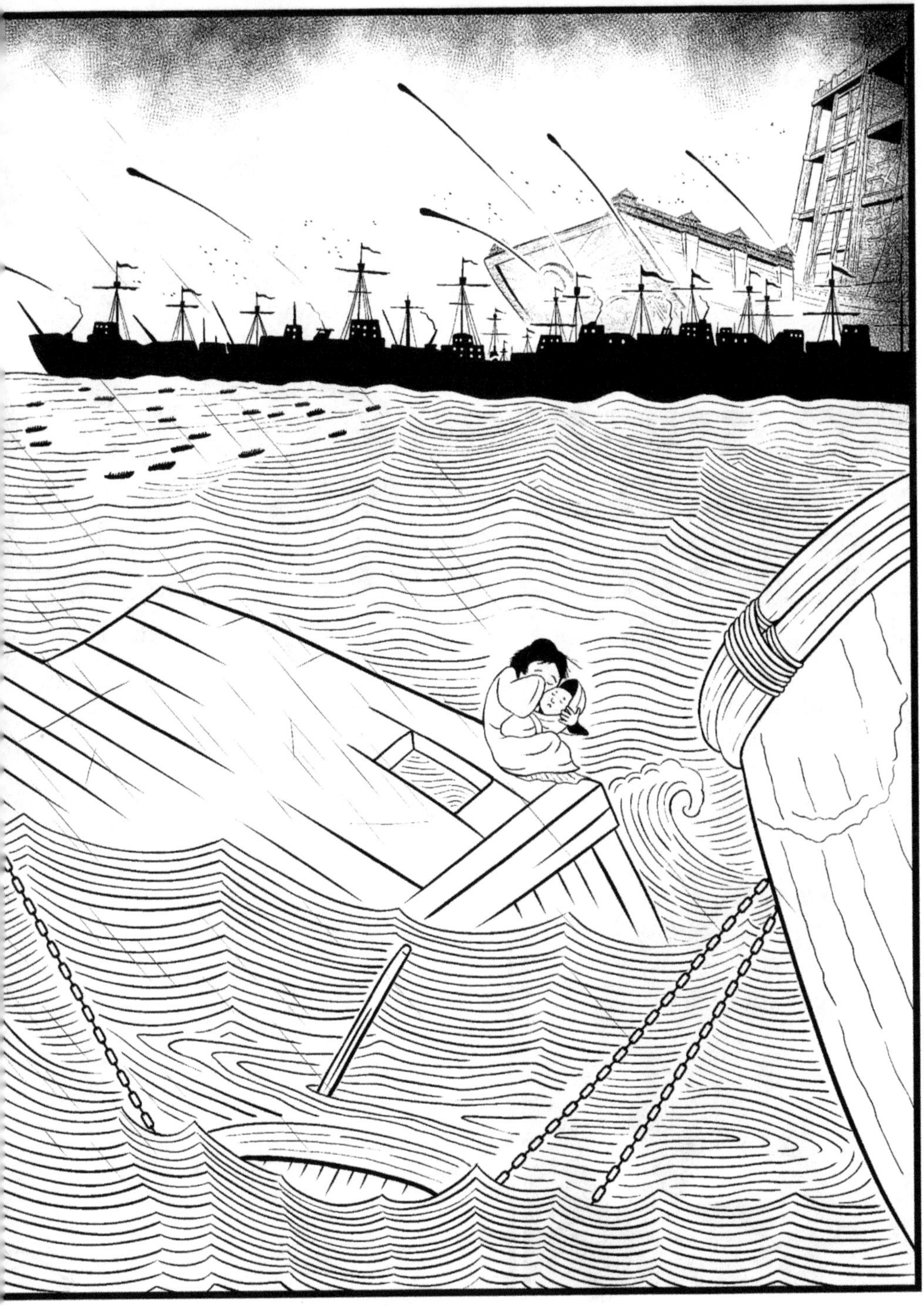

Knowing all was lost, Lu Xiufu went to the emperor.

Today our country is destroyed. Let's not bear even more pain by surrendering.

Lu tied the 8-year-old crying boy and the imperial seal to his back...

...and jumped into the sea, ending the Song dynasty.

The battle of Yamen alone cost the Song Chinese 100,000 lives.

The Mongol conquest had disrupted agriculture, causing widespread famine. The population of China fell from 140 million to 60 million.

Life under Mongol rule

Kublai Khan imposed a military style of rule on his newly conquered subjects.

 No concealed weapons

 No self-organizing

 No public gatherings

 No group worship

 No entertainment after dark

Every household must write down the names of all family members and put that list outside their front gate for inspection.

The Yuan had four social classes:

1   Mongols

2   Miscellaneous ethnic groups,
    including Uyghurs, Tanguts,
    Tibetans, Central Asians,
    Middle Easterners,
    and Europeans

3   Northern Chinese, including
    Khitans and Jurchens

4   Southern barbarians, or
    Chinese of the former
    Southern Song

If a Mongol hits a Chinese,
the Chinese can't fight back.
If the Chinese is beaten to death,
the Mongol is only responsible for
the funeral costs.

Kublai Khan didn't need imperial exams to recruit officials.

Many Chinese intellectuals had to find ways to survive outside the political arena they used to dominate.

They became doctors, private school teachers, writers, artists, and fortunetellers, continuing Chinese cultural traditions independent of Mongol rulers.

Important government positions are reserved for Mongol nobles.

One particularly famous figure from the Yuan dynasty was
Guan Hanqing (1241? – 1320?), considered one of
the greatest playwrights in Chinese history.
He wrote around 60 plays, 14 of which are
still widely read in China today.

Injustice to Dou E

窦娥冤

Rescued by a Coquette

赵盼儿风月
救风尘

In his work, Guan expressed his anger at Mongol rule.

I'm a tough little copper pea
that many have tried to steam, boil, hammer, and stir-fry.
But no one has been able to crack me open.

You can knock out my teeth, mess up my face,
cripple my legs, and break my arms,
but you can never stop me.

Marco Polo

In his distrust of Chinese scholars, Kublai Khan employed foreigners from Central Asia, the Middle East, and Europe to manage the economy and collect taxes.

The Yuan court once put me in charge of salt production in a city in southern China.

Marco Polo (1254 – 1324), a Venetian merchant

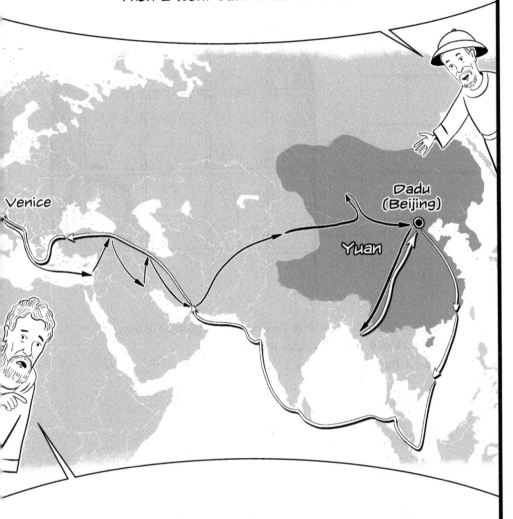

I lived, worked and traveled in China for 17 years.
Then I went back home in 1295.

Upon my return, Venice was at war with another state.
They defeated us and threw me in prison.
There I spent several months telling my story to
a fellow inmate and writer.

His story later became a famous travelogue called
The Travels of Marco Polo.
The book has four parts:

- Journey to China

- China and the Yuan court

- China's neighboring countries

- Wars between different Mongol khanates

This book gave Europeans their first insight into
Chinese politics and people's daily lives.

The original manuscript was lost. Later editions added many errors, which fueled growing suspicion over Marco Polo's tale. Europeans gave the book a nickname: "The Million."

His book is full of exaggerated facts and numbers. It's very hard for us to believe.

Listen to this.

The city of Hangzhou has 12,000 bridges, over 1 million people, and 1.6 million houses!

The Chinese emperor used to live there, and he had thousands of wives, and he raised 20,000 orphans every year.

In a nearby port, there are 15,000 ships docking at 1 wharf.

In Marco polo's book, Venetians also read about Japan for the first time.

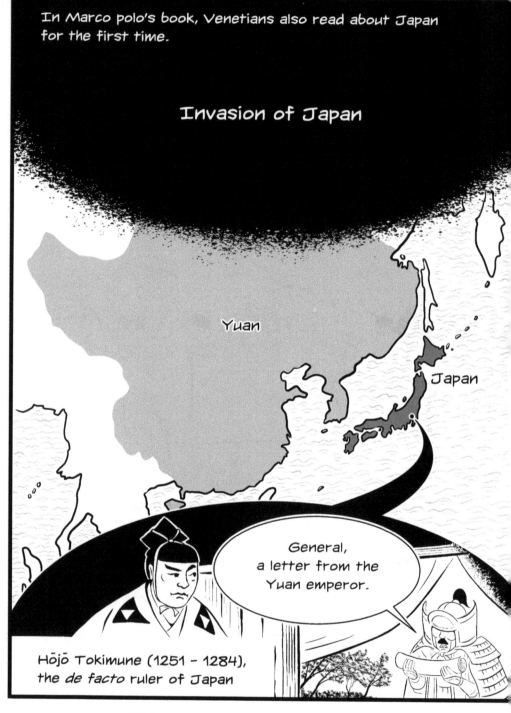

Invasion of Japan

Yuan

Japan

General, a letter from the Yuan emperor.

Hōjō Tokimune (1251 – 1284), the *de facto* ruler of Japan

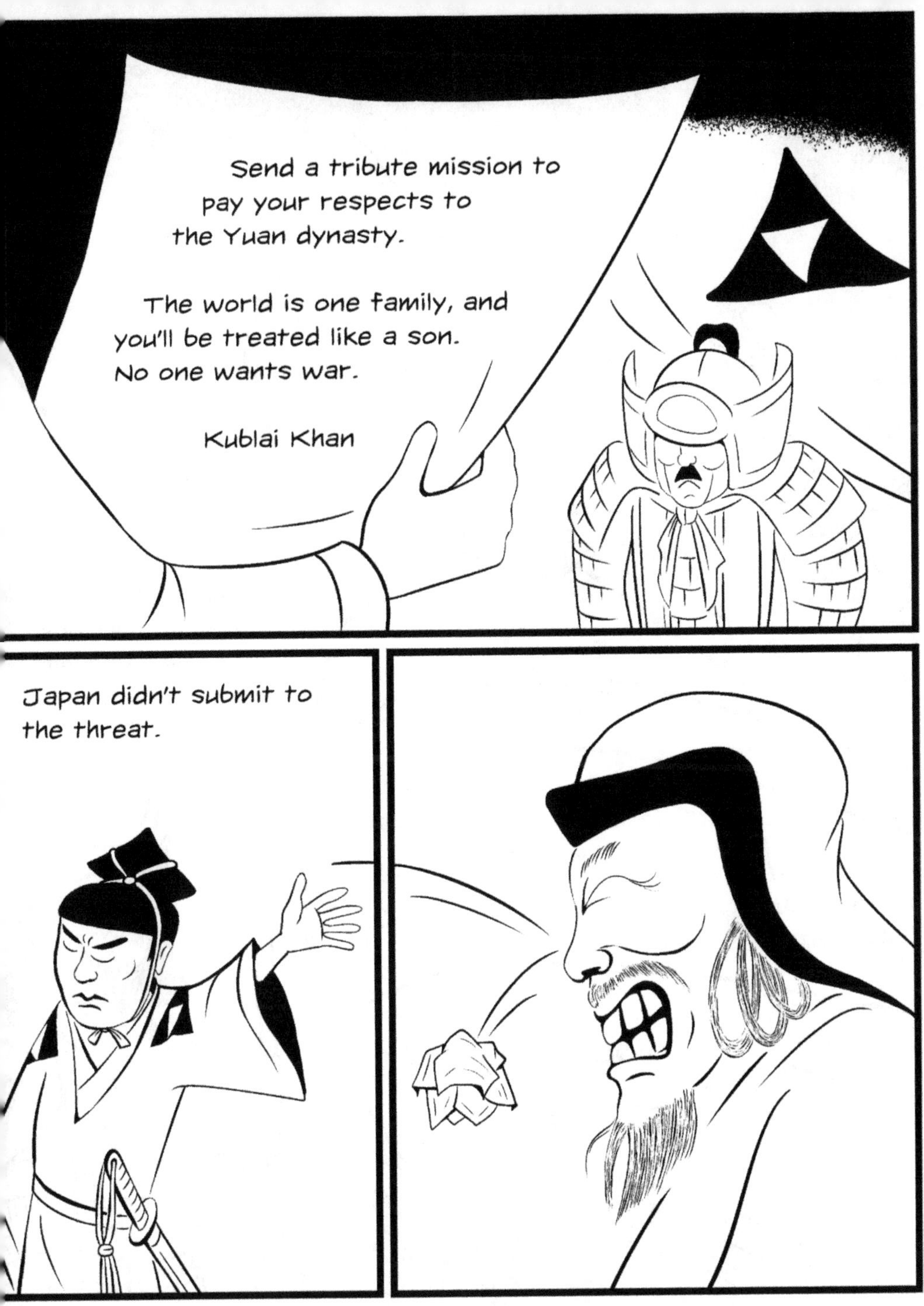

Send a tribute mission to pay your respects to the Yuan dynasty.
The world is one family, and you'll be treated like a son. No one wants war.
Kublai Khan
Japan didn't submit to the threat.

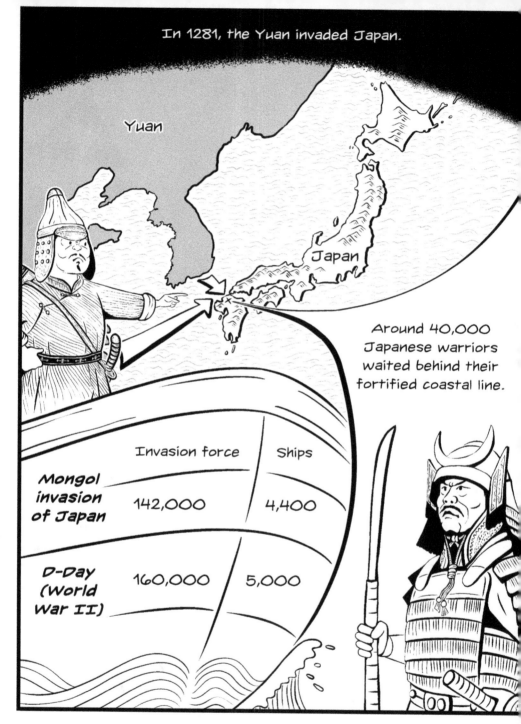

In 1281, the Yuan invaded Japan.

Yuan

Japan

Around 40,000 Japanese warriors waited behind their fortified coastal line.

	Invasion force	Ships
Mongol invasion of Japan	142,000	4,400
D-Day (World War II)	160,000	5,000

After fighting for two months,
the main Yuan army was still unable
to land.

Then came a huge typhoon the Japanese call *Kamikaze**.
Nearly 80% of the Yuan soldiers died.

* In English this means "Divine Wind."

Quick decline

Kublai Khan immediately planned another attack.
Only his own death in 1294 could stop him. The Yuan emperor
left his successors with an age-old question that had troubled
many Chinese leaders.

How to share
power between central and
local governments without
sowing discord?

A Chinese dynasty often built
a strong central government and
treated local authorities as subjects.

Kublai Khan, however, had followed
Mongol tradition and shared power
with family and friends.

This decentralization led to
the rise of many local power centers
that threatened the stability of
the Yuan dynasty.

After Kublai Khan, the Yuan began to decline quickly, weakened by violent struggles between regional factions over succession at the court. Then the Black Death broke out in western Mongol territories, severing all trade between the Yuan and economies to the west.

In 1351 rebellions erupted in southern China. 17 years later, a rebel army captured the Yuan capital, bringing to an end Mongol rule of China.

Chinese civilization survived Mongol rule, but it paid a heavy price.

After the Yuan dynasty, the Chinese had become protective of what they believed was truly, authentically Chinese. They rejected foreign ideas and drifted away from their great tradition of embracing other cultures to enrich their own.

At the same time, explorers like Marco Polo contributed to high demand for Chinese goods in Europe. They also brought back technologies like printing, the compass, and gunpowder. While this exchange of goods and knowledge made important contributions to Europe's technological growth, the blazing pace of Chinese innovation during the Song and Yuan dynasties had come to a halt.

When China clashed with Western countries in the 19th century, it found itself short of ideas to move the country and its people forward. In the words of Li Hongzhang, a leading statesman of the late Qing dynasty, the Chinese had to face "a time of change that we have not seen in thousands of years."

NOTES AND SUGGESTED READING

Pronouncing Chinese names can be very difficult. To keep things as simple as possible I've kept all Chinese names in pinyin, the standard phonetic method for transcribing Chinese words.

The only exceptions are names previously romanized according to different standards that are now very common. An excellent example is the name of the philosopher Confucius. If I were to write it in pinyin it would be spelled *Kong-fuzi*. Instead, I use Confucius, the name Jesuit missionaries gave him in the 16th century.

If you want to check your pinyin pronunciation there are a number of useful online resources available to you. An excellent web dictionary with audio capabilities can be found at www.mdbg.net. The Pleco app for iOS and Android phones allows you to check proper pronunciation.

In writing *Barbarians and the Birth of Chinese Identity* I relied on a number of Chinese-language sources. These include *History of China* by Tongling Wang, *The General History of China* by Simian Lü, *China: A Macro History* by Ray Huang Renyu, and *A History of Chinese Philosophy* by Youlan Feng. Many of these books are classic histories and have more information than I could ever fit into a series, much less a single volume. If you read Chinese these books are worth investigating.

While there aren't a huge number of English-language resources that address the period of Chinese history covered in this book in an accessible manner, *Daily Life in China on the Eve of the Mongol Invasion, 1250 – 1276*, by Jacques Gernet is an excellent resource. I also suggest *Chinese Civilization: A Sourcebook, 2nd Edition*, by Patricia Buckley Ebrey, which collects original source material from Chinese history, including oracle bones, tax codes, and folk tales.

ACKNOWLEDGMENTS

To Sara, Elizabeth, Malcolm and Connor, Katelyn and Yifu, and many, many more children who have been born with a connection to China.

OTHER BOOKS IN THIS SERIES

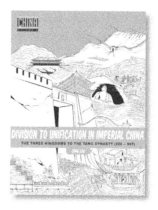

Volume 1
Foundations of Chinese Civilization:
The Yellow Emperor to the Han Dynasty
(2697 BCE – 220 CE)

Volume 2
Division to Unification in Imperial
China: The Three Kingdoms to the Tang
Dynasty (220 – 907)

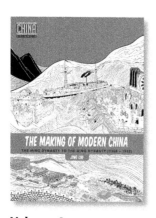

Volume 4
The Making of Modern China: The
Ming Dynasty to the Qing Dynasty
(1368 – 1912)

Volume 5
The Way Forward: From Early Republic
to People's Republic (1912 – 1949)

Printed in the USA
CPSIA information can be obtained
at www.ICGtesting.com
JSHW012054140824
68134JS00035B/3430